LifeSongs

Songbook

Augsburg Fortress
Minneapolis

LIFESONGS Songbook

Also available:
LifeSongs Leader Book (11-10939) ISBN 0-8066-4270-X
LifeSongs compact discs
   Volume 1 ages 3 and up (11-10941) ISBN 0-8066-4272-6
   Volume 2 ages 7 and up (11-10942) ISBN 0-8066-4273-4

The paper used in this publication meets the minimum requirements of American National Standard for Information Sciences—Permanence of Paper for Printed Materials, ANSI Z329.48-1984.

Manufactured in the U.S.A.   ISBN 0-8066-4271-8   11-10940

05 04 03 02 01 00   3 4 5 6 7 8 9 10

Table of contents

Preface

Hymns and Songs

Indexes

Preface

To sing of faith is to sing of the life that is God's gift. *LifeSongs* opens new avenues of exploration through which children of various ages may discover the ways that their lives are a song to God. This resource links music, education, and worship so that children may grow in and celebrate their life together with God, with one another, and with the church.

LifeSongs gathers musical items carefully selected to meet the needs of children from early through later childhood years, for use in learning, worship, recreational, and home environments. Included here are traditional and new children's songs, call and response songs, rounds and action songs, scripture songs, contemporary worship songs, songs from various cultures, as well as representative hymns, carols, and refrains of the church and its liturgy.

The *LifeSongs* **songbook**, containing words and melody lines only, can be placed directly into the hands of singers. The *LifeSongs* **leader book** contains a variety of helpful features for teachers and other leaders: practical methods of teaching the songs, background information, full accompaniments, and an appendix of early childhood song texts (#190–200, not included in this songbook) for use with nursery and folk tunes. In addition to these two print resources, *LifeSongs* **recordings** include a representative selection of songs both for younger children (ages 3 and up) and older children (ages 7 and up).

LifeSongs is a musical companion to the materials in the Life Together family of resources available from Augsburg Fortress. The three-year lectionary and the seasons of the church year are important organizing principles for these resources. The *LifeSongs* package, however, is also recommended for use independently, wherever churches are seeking to encourage children to sing. As they listen, move, play, sing, and pray together, children who encounter these songs can begin to build their own understanding of the Christian story, enjoy the life they share with all God's children, and develop a lifelong love for lifting their voices in worship and song.

Stay awake, be ready

1 Stay a - wake, *(clap, clap)* be read - y. You
2 Change your lives, he's com - ing. The
3 Go. . . . back, tell John
4 By the pow'r of the Spir - it

do not know the hour when the Lord is com - ing. Stay a -
one who is the light of the world is com - ing. Change your
all that you have heard and have seen me do - ing. Go . . . .
Mar - y will give birth to a son called Je - sus. By the

wake, be read - y. The Lord is com - ing soon!
lives, he's com - ing. The reign of God is near!
back, tell John the won - ders that you see.
pow'r of the Spir - it Em - man - u - el is near.

Al - le - lu - ia, al - le - lu - ia!
The Lord is com - ing soon.
The reign of God is near.
The won - ders that you see.
Em - man - u - el is near.

Text: Christopher Walker
Music: Christopher Walker

2

Soon and very soon

1 Soon and ver - y soon
2 No more cry - in' there,
3 No more dy - in' there,
4 Soon and ver - y soon
we are goin' to see the King,

soon and ver - y soon
no more cry - in' there,
no more dy - in' there,
soon and ver - y soon
we are goin' to see the King,

soon and ver - y soon
no more cry - in' there,
no more dy - in' there,
soon and ver - y soon
we are goin' to see the King.

1, 2
Hal-le - lu - jah, hal-le - lu - jah, we're goin' to see the King!

3, 4
Hal - le - lu - jah, hal - le - lu -

jah, hal - le - lu - jah, hal - le - lu - jah.

Text: Andraé Crouch
Music: Andraé Crouch

© 1976 Bud John Songs, Inc./Crouch Music, admin. EMI Christian Music Publishing

Light one candle: Christ is coming
3

Advent candle song

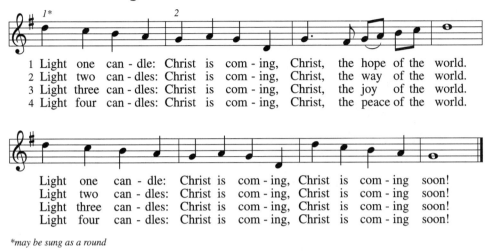

1 Light one can-dle: Christ is com-ing, Christ, the hope of the world.
2 Light two can-dles: Christ is com-ing, Christ, the way of the world.
3 Light three can-dles: Christ is com-ing, Christ, the joy of the world.
4 Light four can-dles: Christ is com-ing, Christ, the peace of the world.

Light one can-dle: Christ is com-ing, Christ is com-ing soon!
Light two can-dles: Christ is com-ing, Christ is com-ing soon!
Light three can-dles: Christ is com-ing, Christ is com-ing soon!
Light four can-dles: Christ is com-ing, Christ is com-ing soon!

*may be sung as a round

Text: Sally Ahner
Music: Sally Ahner
© 1992 Abingdon Press, admin. The Copyright Company

He came down
4

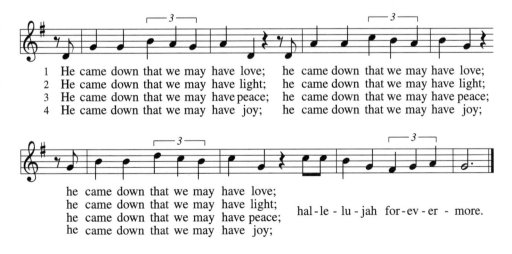

1 He came down that we may have love; he came down that we may have love;
2 He came down that we may have light; he came down that we may have light;
3 He came down that we may have peace; he came down that we may have peace;
4 He came down that we may have joy; he came down that we may have joy;

he came down that we may have love;
he came down that we may have light;
he came down that we may have peace;
he came down that we may have joy;

hal-le-lu-jah for-ev-er-more.

Text: Cameroon traditional
Music: Cameroon traditional

5

The King shall come

1 The King shall come when morn - ing dawns and
2 Not as of old a lit - tle child, to
3 Oh, bright - er than the ris - ing morn when
4 Oh, bright - er than that glo - rious morn shall
5 The King shall come when morn - ing dawns and

light tri - um - phant breaks, when beau - ty gilds the
bear and fight and die, but crowned with glo - ry
Christ, vic - to - rious, rose and left the lone - some
dawn up - on our race the day when Christ in
light and beau - ty brings. Hail, Christ the Lord! Your

east - ern hills and life to joy a - wakes.
like the sun that lights the morn - ing sky.
place of death, de - spite the rage of foes.
splen - dor comes, and we shall see his face.
peo - ple pray: come quick - ly, King of kings.

Text: John Brownlie
Music: A. Davisson, *Kentucky Harmony*

On Jordan's banks the Baptist's cry

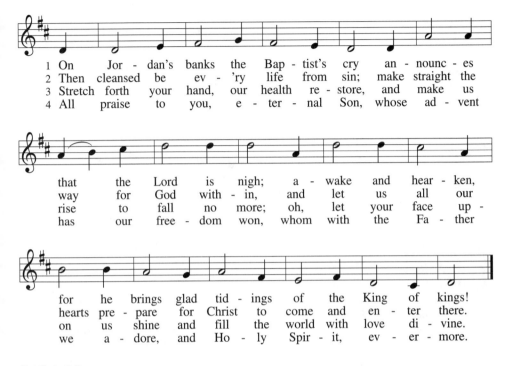

1 On Jor - dan's banks the Bap - tist's cry an - nounc - es
2 Then cleansed be ev - 'ry life from sin; make straight the
3 Stretch forth your hand, our health re - store, and make us
4 All praise to you, e - ter - nal Son, whose ad - vent

that the Lord is nigh; a - wake and hear - ken,
way for God with - in, and let us all our
rise to fall no more; oh, let your face up -
has our free - dom won, whom with the Fa - ther

for he brings glad tid - ings of the King of kings!
hearts pre - pare for Christ to come and en - ter there.
on us shine and fill the world with love di - vine.
we a - dore, and Ho - ly Spir - it, ev - er - more.

Text: Charles Coffin
Music: European tune, adapt. Michael Praetorius

7

Prepare the royal highway

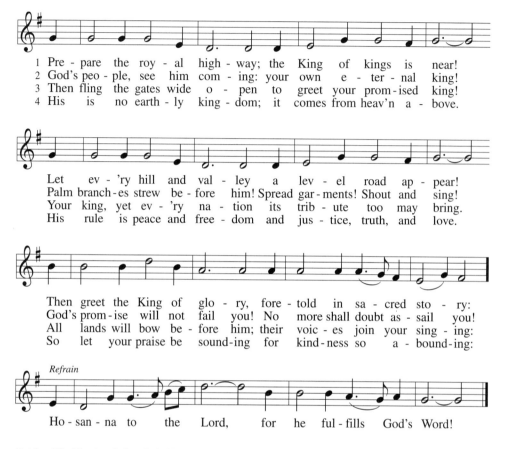

1 Pre - pare the roy - al high - way; the King of kings is near!
2 God's peo - ple, see him com - ing: your own e - ter - nal king!
3 Then fling the gates wide o - pen to greet your prom - ised king!
4 His is no earth - ly king - dom; it comes from heav'n a - bove.

Let ev - 'ry hill and val - ley a lev - el road ap - pear!
Palm branch - es strew be - fore him! Spread gar - ments! Shout and sing!
Your king, yet ev - 'ry na - tion its trib - ute too may bring.
His rule is peace and free - dom and jus - tice, truth, and love.

Then greet the King of glo - ry, fore - told in sa - cred sto - ry:
God's prom - ise will not fail you! No more shall doubt as - sail you!
All lands will bow be - fore him; their voic - es join your sing - ing:
So let your praise be sound - ing for kind - ness so a - bound - ing:

Refrain

Ho - san - na to the Lord, for he ful - fills God's Word!

Text: Frans Mikael Franzén; tr. *Lutheran Book of Worship*
Music: Swedish traditional
Tr. © 1978 *Lutheran Book of Worship*

The King of glory

Refrain

The King of glo - ry comes, the na - tion re - joic - es.

O - pen the gates be - fore him, lift up your voic - es.

1 Who is the King of glo - ry; how shall we call him?
2 In all of Gal - i - lee, in cit - y or vil - lage,
3 Sing then of Da - vid's Son, our Sav - ior and broth - er;
4 He gave his life for us, the pledge of sal - va - tion;
5 He con - quered sin and death; he tru - ly has ris - en,

Refrain

He is Em - man - u - el, the prom - ised of ag - es.
he goes a - mong his peo - ple, cur - ing their ill - ness.
in all of Gal - i - lee was nev - er an - oth - er.
he took up - on him - self the sins of the na - tion.
and he will share with us his heav - en - ly vi - sion.

Text: Willard F. Jabusch
Music: Israeli traditional
Text © 1968, 1982 Willard F. Jabusch, admin. OCP Publications

9

We light the Advent candles

1 We light the Ad-vent can - dles a - gainst the win - ter night
2 The first one will re - mind us that Christ will soon re - turn.
3 We light the sec - ond can - dle, and hear God's ho - ly word.
4 Three can - dles now are gleam - ing and show us the true way.
5 Four can - dles burn-ing bright - ly an - nounce that Christ has come.

to wel-come our Lord Je - sus, who is the world's true light;
We light it in the dark - ness and watch it gleam and burn.
It tells us, cling to Je - sus, pre - pare to meet your Lord.
Re - joice, the Bap - tist cries out: your Lord has come to - day!
Pre - pare, my heart, be - lieve it, and give the Christ child room!

to wel-come our Lord Je - sus, who is the world's true light.
We light it in the dark - ness and watch it gleam and burn.
It tells us, cling to Je - sus, pre - pare to meet your Lord.
Re - joice, the Bap - tist cries out: your Lord has come to - day!
Pre - pare, my heart, be - lieve it, and give the Christ child room!

Text: Gracia Grindal
Music: German traditional
Text © 1999 Hope Publishing Company

Oh, come, oh, come, Emmanuel

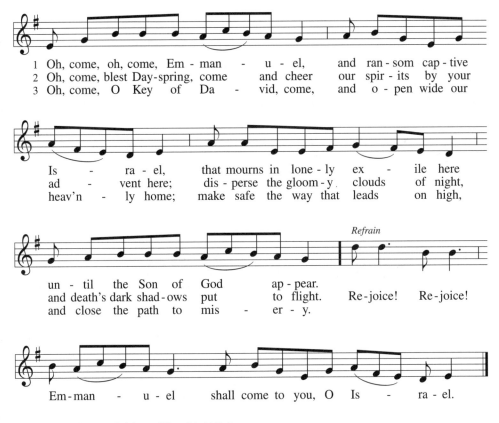

1 Oh, come, oh, come, Em-man - u - el, and ran-som cap-tive
2 Oh, come, blest Day-spring, come and cheer our spir-its by your
3 Oh, come, O Key of Da - vid, come, and o-pen wide our

Is - ra - el, that mourns in lone-ly ex - ile here
ad - vent here; dis-perse the gloom-y clouds of night,
heav'n - ly home; make safe the way that leads on high,

Refrain

un - til the Son of God ap-pear.
and death's dark shad-ows put to flight. Re-joice! Re-joice!
and close the path to mis - er - y.

Em-man - u - el shall come to you, O Is - ra - el.

Text: *Psalteriolum Cantionum Catholicarum*, Köln; tr. John M. Neale
Music: French processional

11

People, look east

1. Peo - ple, look east. The time is near of the
   crown-ing of the year. Make your house fair as you are
   a - ble, trim the hearth and set the ta - ble. Peo-ple look
   east, and sing to - day— Love, the Guest, is on the way.

2. Fur - rows, be glad. Though earth is bare, one more
   seed is plant - ed there. Give up your strength the seed to
   nour - ish, that in course the flower may flour - ish. Peo-ple, look
   east, and sing to - day— Love, the Rose, is on the way.

3. Stars, keep the watch. When night is dim, one more
   light the bowl shall brim, shin - ing be - yond the frost - y
   weath - er, bright as sun and moon to - geth - er. Peo-ple, look
   east, and sing to - day— Love, the Star, is on the way.

4. An - gels an - nounce with shouts of mirth him who
   brings new life to earth. Set ev - 'ry peak and val - ley
   hum - ming with the word, the Lord is com - ing. Peo-ple, look
   east, and sing to - day— Love, the Lord, is on the way.

Text: Eleanor Farjeon
Music: French carol
Text © 1931 Eleanor Farjeon, admin. David Higham Associates, Ltd.

Get ready! 12

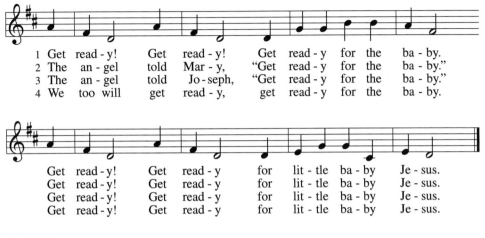

1 Get read - y! Get read - y! Get read - y for the ba - by.
2 The an - gel told Mar - y, "Get read - y for the ba - by."
3 The an - gel told Jo - seph, "Get read - y for the ba - by."
4 We too will get read - y, get read - y for the ba - by.

Get read - y! Get read - y for lit - tle ba - by Je - sus.
Get read - y! Get read - y for lit - tle ba - by Je - sus.
Get read - y! Get read - y for lit - tle ba - by Je - sus.
Get read - y! Get read - y for lit - tle ba - by Je - sus.

Text: Linda Carpenter
Music: Lois Holck

© 1985 Parish Life Press, admin. Augsburg Fortress

Come now, O Prince of Peace 13

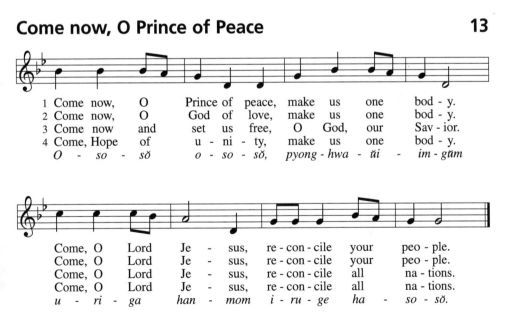

1 Come now, O Prince of peace, make us one bod - y.
2 Come now, O God of love, make us one bod - y.
3 Come now and set us free, O God, our Sav - ior.
4 Come, Hope of u - ni - ty, make us one bod - y.
O - so - sŏ o - so - sŏ, pyong - hwa - ŭi - im - gŭm

Come, O Lord Je - sus, re - con - cile your peo - ple.
Come, O Lord Je - sus, re - con - cile your peo - ple.
Come, O Lord Je - sus, re - con - cile all na - tions.
Come, O Lord Je - sus, re - con - cile all na - tions.
u - ri - ga han - mom i - ru - ge ha - so - sŏ.

Text: Geonyong Lee; tr. Marion Pope
Music: Korean traditional

Text © Geonyong Lee
Tr. © Marion Pope

14   # That boy-child of Mary

Refrain

That boy-child of Mar - y was born in a sta - ble,

a man - ger his cra - dle in Beth - le - hem.

1 What shall we call him, child of the man - ger?
2 His name is Je - sus, God ev - er with us,
3 How can he save us, how can he help us,
4 Gift of the Fa - ther, to hu - man moth - er,

Refrain

What name is giv - en in Beth - le - hem?
God giv - en for us in Beth - le - hem.
born here a - mong us in Beth - le - hem?
makes him our broth - er in Beth - le - hem.

5   One with the Father,
    he is our Savior,
    heaven-sent helper
    in Bethlehem. *Refrain*

6   Gladly we praise him,
    love and adore him,
    give ourselves to him
    in Bethlehem. *Refrain*

Text: Tom Colvin
Music: Malawian traditional, adapt. Tom Colvin
© 1969 Hope Publishing Company

'Twas in the moon of wintertime

1 'Twas in the moon of win-ter-time when all the birds had fled,
2 The ear-liest moon of win-ter-time is not so round and fair
3 O chil-dren of the for-est free, the an-gels' song is true.

that God, the Lord of all the earth, sent an-gel choirs in-stead.
as was the ring of glo - ry a-round the in-fant there.
The ho-ly child of earth and heav'n is born to-day for you.

Be - fore their light the stars grew dim, and wan-d'ring hunt-ers
And when the shep-herds then drew near the an-gel voic-es
Come, kneel be-fore the ra - diant boy, who brings you beau-ty,

Refrain

heard the hymn:
rang out clear: Je - sus your king is born!
peace and joy.

Je - sus is born! Glo-ry be to God on high!

Text: Jean de Brebeuf; tr. Jesse E. Middleton, alt.
Music: French traditional
Tr. © 1927 Frederick Harris Co., Ltd.

16
Angels we have heard on high

1 An - gels we have heard on high, sweet - ly sing - ing o'er the plains,
2 Shep-herds, why this ju - bi - lee? Why your joy - ous strains pro-long?
3 Come to Beth - le - hem and see him whose birth the an - gels sing;

and the moun-tains in re - ply, ech - o - ing their joy - ous strains.
What the glad-some tid - ings be which in - spire your heav'n - ly song?
come, a - dore on bend - ed knee Christ the Lord, the new - born king.

Refrain

Glo - - - ri - a

in ex - cel - sis De - o; glo - -

- - ri - a in ex - cel - sis De - o.

Text: French carol; tr. "Crown of Jesus"
Music: French carol

Away in a manger
17

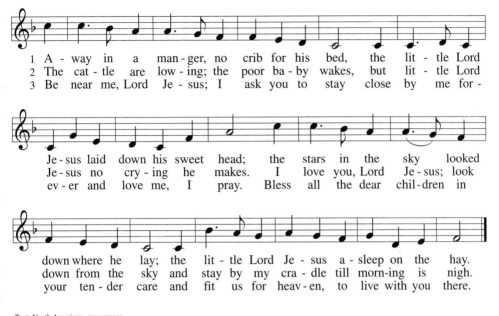

1 A - way in a man-ger, no crib for his bed, the lit - tle Lord
2 The cat - tle are low - ing; the poor ba - by wakes, but lit - tle Lord
3 Be near me, Lord Je - sus; I ask you to stay close by me for -

Je - sus laid down his sweet head; the stars in the sky looked
Je - sus no cry - ing he makes. I love you, Lord Je - sus; look
ev - er and love me, I pray. Bless all the dear chil - dren in

down where he lay; the lit - tle Lord Je - sus a - sleep on the hay.
down from the sky and stay by my cra - dle till morn - ing is nigh.
your ten - der care and fit us for heav - en, to live with you there.

Text: North American, anonymous
Music: North American, anonymous

Away in a manger
18

1 A - way in a man - ger, no crib for his bed, the lit - tle Lord
2 The cat - tle are low - ing; the poor ba - by wakes, but lit - tle Lord
3 Be near me, Lord Je - sus; I ask you to stay close by me for -

Je - sus laid down his sweet head; the stars in the bright sky looked
Je - sus no cry - ing he makes. I love you, Lord Je - sus; look
ev - er and love me, I pray. Bless all the dear chil - dren in

down where he lay; the lit - tle Lord Je - sus a - sleep on the hay.
down from the sky and stay by my cra - dle till morn - ing is nigh.
your ten - der care and fit us for heav - en, to live with you there.

Text: North American, anonymous
Music: William J. Kirkpatrick

19   Sing we now of Jesus

Christmas: Sing we now of Je - sus, born on Christ-mas day.
Easter: Sing we now of Je - sus, ris'n on Eas - ter day.

Sing we now of Je - sus, born on bed of hay.
Sing we now of Je - sus, ris'n from death's dark grave.

Lift up your voice, with all the world re - joice;
Lift up your voice, with all the world re - joice;

sing we now of Je - sus, born to light our way.
sing we now of Je - sus, ris'n the world to save.

*may be sung as a round

Text: Michael Burkhardt
Music: French carol
Text © 1995 MorningStar Music Publishers

20   Glory to God

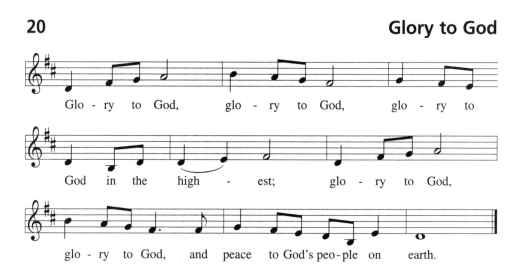

Glo - ry to God, glo - ry to God, glo - ry to

God in the high - est; glo - ry to God,

glo - ry to God, and peace to God's peo - ple on earth.

Text: "Gloria," tr. English Language Liturgical Consultation
Music: Jeremy Young
Music © 1995 Augsburg Fortress

Gloria
21

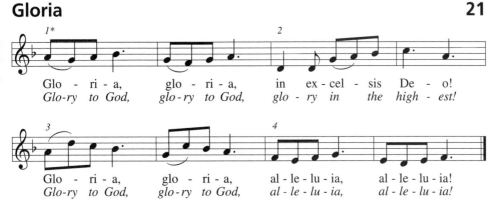

Glo - ri - a, glo - ri - a, in ex - cel - sis De - o!
Glo-ry to God, glo-ry to God, glo - ry in the high - est!

Glo - ri - a, glo - ri - a, al - le - lu - ia, al - le - lu - ia!
Glo-ry to God, glo-ry to God, al - le - lu - ia, al - le - lu - ia!

*may be sung as a round

Text: traditional
Music: Jacques Berthier
Music © 1988 Les Presses de Taizé, admin. GIA Publications, Inc.

I am so glad each Christmas Eve
22

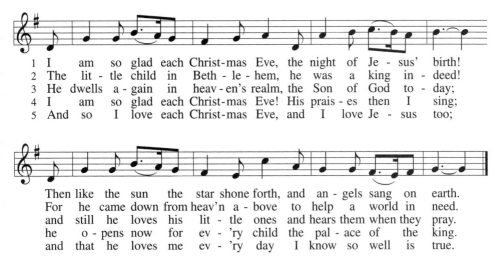

1 I am so glad each Christ-mas Eve, the night of Je - sus' birth!
2 The lit - tle child in Beth - le - hem, he was a king in - deed!
3 He dwells a - gain in heav - en's realm, the Son of God to - day;
4 I am so glad each Christ-mas Eve! His prais - es then I sing;
5 And so I love each Christ-mas Eve, and I love Je - sus too;

Then like the sun the star shone forth, and an - gels sang on earth.
For he came down from heav'n a - bove to help a world in need.
and still he loves his lit - tle ones and hears them when they pray.
he o - pens now for ev - 'ry child the pal - ace of the king.
and that he loves me ev - 'ry day I know so well is true.

Text: Marie Wexelsen; tr. Peter A. Sveeggen, alt.
Music: Peder Knudsen
Tr. © 1932 Augsburg Publishing House

23 # Go tell it on the mountain

Refrain

Go tell it on the moun-tain, o-ver the hills and ev-'ry-where;

go tell it on the moun-tain that Je-sus Christ is born!

1 While shep-herds kept their watch-ing o'er si-lent flocks by night,
2 The shep-herds feared and trem-bled when, lo, a-bove the earth
3 Down in a lone-ly man-ger the hum-ble Christ was born;

Refrain

be-hold, through-out the heav-ens there shone a ho-ly light.
rang out the an-gel cho-rus that hailed our Sav-ior's birth.
and God sent us sal-va-tion that bless-ed Christ-mas morn.

Text: African American spiritual, refrain; John W. Work, Jr., stanzas
Music: African American spiritual

Joy to the world

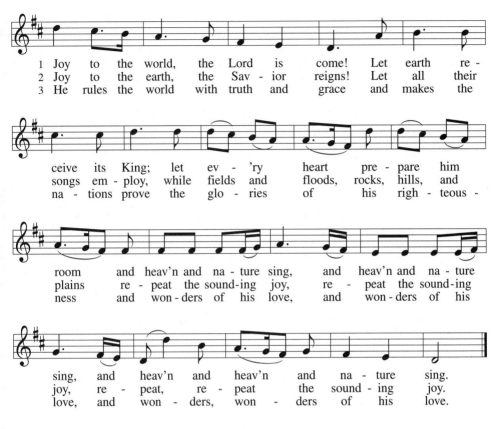

1 Joy to the world, the Lord is come! Let earth re-
2 Joy to the earth, the Sav - ior reigns! Let all their
3 He rules the world with truth and grace and makes the

ceive its King; let ev - 'ry heart pre - pare him
songs em - ploy, while fields and floods, rocks, hills, and
na - tions prove the glo - ries of his righ - teous -

room and heav'n and na - ture sing, and heav'n and na - ture
plains re - peat the sound-ing joy, re - peat the sound-ing
ness and won - ders of his love, and won - ders of his

sing, and heav'n and heav'n and na - ture sing.
joy, re - peat, re - peat the sound - ing joy.
love, and won - ders, won - ders of his love.

Text: Isaac Watts
Music: George F. Handel, adapt.

25 Hark! The herald angels sing

1 Hark! The her - ald an - gels sing, "Glo - ry to the new-born king;
2 Hail the heav'n - born Prince of Peace! Hail the sun of right-teous-ness!

peace on earth, and mer-cy mild, God and sin - ners rec - on - ciled."
Light and life to all he brings, ris'n with heal - ing in his wings.

Joy - ful, all you na-tions, rise; join the tri-umph of the skies;
Mild he lays his glo - ry by, born that we no more may die,

with an - gel - ic hosts pro-claim, "Christ is born in Beth - le - hem!"
born to raise each child of earth, born to give us sec - ond birth.

Refrain

Hark! The her - ald an-gels sing, "Glo - ry to the new-born king!"

Text: Charles Wesley, alt.
Music: Felix Mendelssohn

Silent night, holy night!

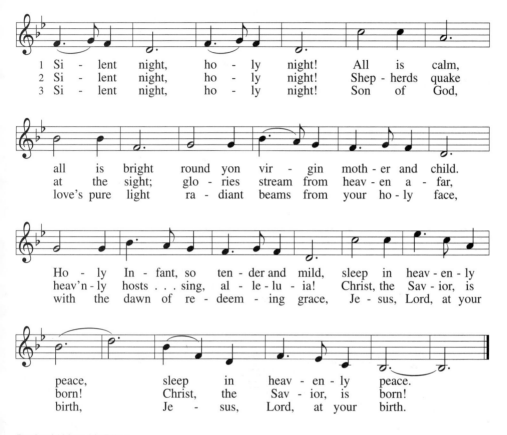

1 Si - lent night, ho - ly night! All is calm,
2 Si - lent night, ho - ly night! Shep - herds quake
3 Si - lent night, ho - ly night! Son of God,

all is bright round yon vir - gin moth - er and child.
at the sight; glo - ries stream from heav - en a - far,
love's pure light ra - diant beams from your ho - ly face,

Ho - ly In - fant, so ten - der and mild, sleep in heav - en - ly
heav'n - ly hosts . . . sing, al - le - lu - ia! Christ, the Sav - ior, is
with the dawn of re - deem - ing grace, Je - sus, Lord, at your

peace, sleep in heav - en - ly peace.
born! Christ, the Sav - ior, is born!
birth, Je - sus, Lord, at your birth.

Text: Joseph Mohr; tr. John F. Young
Music: Franz Gruber

27 Oh, come, all ye faithful

1 Oh, come, all ye faith - ful, joy - ful and tri - um - phant! Oh,
2 Sing, choirs of an - gels, sing in ex - ul - ta - tion, . . .
3 Yea, Lord, we greet thee, born this hap - py morn - ing; . . .

come ye, oh, come ye to Beth - le - hem;
sing, all ye cit - i - zens of heav - en a - bove!
Je - sus, to thee be . . . glo - ry giv'n!

come and be - hold him, born the king of an - gels:
Glo - ry to God . . . . in . . . the . . . high - est:
Word of the Fa - ther, now in flesh ap - pear - ing:

Refrain

Oh, come, let us a - dore him, oh, come, let us a - dore him,

oh, come, let us a - dore him, Christ the Lord!

Text: attr. John F. Wade, tr. Frederick Oakeley
Music: attr. John F. Wade

Oh, sleep now, holy baby

1 Oh, sleep now, ho - ly ba - by, with your head a - gainst my breast;
1 *Duér - me - te, ni - ño lin - do, en los bra - zos del a - mor*

mean-while the pangs of my sor - row are soothed and put to rest.
mien - tras que duer - me_y des - can - sa la pe - na de mi do - lor.

Refrain/Estribillo

A la ru, a la mé, a la ru, a la mé,

a la ru, a la mé, a la ru, a la ru, a la mé.

2 You need not fear King Herod,
  he will bring no harm to you;
  so rest in the arms of your mother
  who sings you a la ru. *Refrain*

2 *No temas al rey Herodes*
  que nada te_ha de hacer;
  en los brazos de tu madre
  y_ahi nadie te_ha de_ofender. Estribillo

Text: Hispanic folk song; tr. John Donald Robb
Music: Hispanic folk tune; arr. John Donald Robb
Translation and arr. © 1954 University of New Mexico Foundation, Robb Musical Trust

29 The virgin Mary had a baby boy

1 The vir - gin Mar - y had a ba - by boy, the
2 The an - gels sang . . . when the ba - by was born, the
3 The shep - herds came . . . . where the ba - by was born, the
4 The wise men saw . . . where the ba - by was born, the

vir - gin Mar - y had a ba-by boy, the vir - gin Mar - y had a
an - gels sang . . . when the ba-by was born, the an - gels sang . . when the
shep-herds came . . . where the ba-by was born, the shep-herds came . . where the
wise men saw . . . where the ba-by was born, the wise men saw . . where the

ba - by boy, and they say that his name is Je - sus.
ba - by was born, and they sang that his name is Je - sus.
ba - by was born, and they say that the virgin Mar - y had a
ba - by was born, and they say that his name is Je - sus.

Refrain

He come from the glo - ry, he come from the glo-rious king-dom.

He come from the glo - ry, he come from the glo-rious king-dom.

Oh, yes, be - liev - er! Oh, yes, be - liev - er! He come from the

glo - ry, he come from the glo - rious king-dom.

Text: West Indian carol
Music: West Indian carol; arr. John Barnard
© 1945 Boosey and Company, Ltd., admin. Boosey and Hawkes, Inc.

We three kings of Orient are

1 We three kings of O - ri - ent are; bear - ing
2 Born a king on Beth - le - hem's plain, gold I
3 Frank - in - cense to of - fer have I; in - cense
4 Myrrh is mine; its bit - ter per - fume breathes a
5 Glo - rious now be - hold him a - rise, King and

gifts we tra - verse a - far, field and foun - tain,
bring to crown him a - gain; king for - ev - er,
owns a de - i - ty nigh; prayer and prais - ing,
life of gath - er - ing gloom; sor - rowing, sigh - ing,
God and Sac - ri - fice; heav'n sings al - le -

moor and moun - tain, fol - low - ing yon - der star.
ceas - ing nev - er, o - ver us all to reign.
glad - ly rais - ing, wor - ship - ing God Most High.
bleed - ing, dy - ing, sealed in the stone - cold tomb.
lu - ia: al - le - lu - ia the earth re - plies.

Refrain

Oh, star of won - der, star of night, star with roy - al beau - ty bright;

west - ward lead - ing, still pro - ceed - ing, guide us to thy per - fect light!

Text: John Henry Hopkins, Jr.
Music: John Henry Hopkins, Jr.

31

Open our eyes, Lord

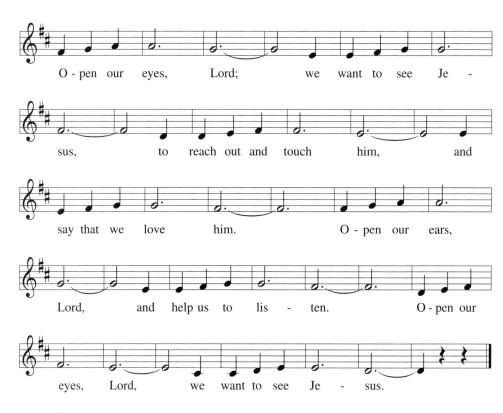

O - pen our eyes, Lord; we want to see Je -

sus, to reach out and touch him, and

say that we love him. O - pen our ears,

Lord, and help us to lis - ten. O - pen our

eyes, Lord, we want to see Je - sus.

Text: Bob Cull
Music: Bob Cull
© 1976 Maranatha! Music, admin. The Copyright Company

This little light of mine

1 This lit - tle light of mine, I'm goin' - a let it shine;

this lit - tle light of mine, I'm goin' - a let it shine,

Refrain

let it shine, let it shine, let it shine.

Fine

2 Hide it un - der a bas - ket? No! I'm goin' - a let it
3 Don't let a - ny - one *(blow)* it out. I'm goin' - a let it
4 Share my light with . . . oth - ers! Yes! I'm goin' - a let it

Refrain

shine. Hide it un - der a bas - ket? No!
shine. Don't let a - ny - one *(blow)* it out.
shine. Share my light with . . . oth - ers! Yes!

Text: traditional
Music: traditional

33

This little light of mine

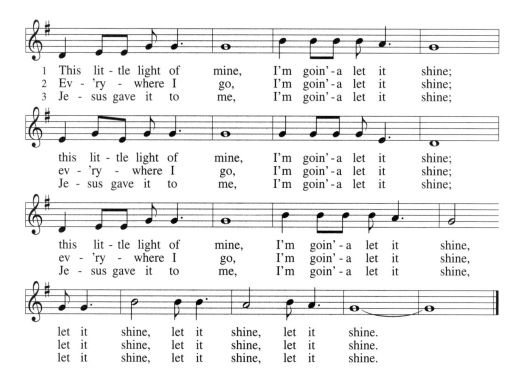

1 This lit - tle light of mine, I'm goin' - a let it shine;
2 Ev - 'ry - where I go, I'm goin' - a let it shine;
3 Je - sus gave it to me, I'm goin' - a let it shine;

this lit - tle light of mine, I'm goin' - a let it shine;
ev - 'ry - where I go, I'm goin' - a let it shine;
Je - sus gave it to me, I'm goin' - a let it shine;

this lit - tle light of mine, I'm goin' - a let it shine,
ev - 'ry - where I go, I'm goin' - a let it shine,
Je - sus gave it to me, I'm goin' - a let it shine,

let it shine, let it shine, let it shine.
let it shine, let it shine, let it shine.
let it shine, let it shine, let it shine.

Text: African American spiritual
Music: African American spiritual

34

I am the light of the world

I am the light of the world, I am the light of the world. Who-

ev - er fol-lows me will nev-er walk in the dark, will nev-er

walk in the dark, but have the light of life.

Text: John 8:12
Music: June Fischer Armstrong

Bring forth the kingdom

Leader

1 You are   salt for the earth, O peo-ple: salt   for the king-dom of God!
2 You are a light on the   hill, O peo-ple: light for the cit - y of God!
3 You are a seed of the word, O peo-ple: bring forth the king-dom of God!
4 We are a blest and a   pil-grim peo-ple: bound for the king-dom of God!

Leader   **All**

Share the fla-vor of   life, O peo-ple: life in the king-dom of God!
Shine so ho - ly and bright, O peo-ple: shine for the king-dom of God!
Seeds of mer-cy and seeds of jus-tice, grow in the king-dom of God!
Love our jour-ney and love our home-land: love is the king-dom of God!

Refrain

Bring   forth   the   king-dom of   mer - cy,   bring   forth   the

king-dom of peace;   bring   forth   the   king-dom of jus - tice,

bring   forth   the   cit - y   of   God!

Text: Marty Haugen
Music: Marty Haugen
© 1986 GIA Publications

36   I want to walk as a child of the light

1 I want to walk as a child of the light.
2 I want to see ... the bright - ness of God.
3 I'm look - ing for ... the com - ing of Christ.

I want to fol - low Je - sus.
I want to look at Je - sus.
I want to be with Je - sus.

God set the stars to give light to the world.
Clear Sun of righ - teous - ness, shine on my path,
When we have run .... with pa - tience the race,

The star of my life is Je - sus.
and show me the way to the Fa - ther.
we shall know the joy of Je - sus.

Refrain

In him there is no dark - ness at all. The night and the

day are both a - like. The Lamb is the light of the

cit - y of God. Shine in my heart, Lord Je - sus.

Text: Kathleen Thomerson
Music: Kathleen Thomerson
© 1970 Celebration, admin. The Copyright Company

We are called

1 Come! Live in the light!
2 Come! O - pen your heart!
3 Sing! Sing a new song!

Shine with the joy and the love of the Lord! We are
Show your... mer - cy to all those in fear! We are
Sing of that great day when all will be one! God will

called to be light for the king - dom, to
called to be hope for the hope - less so all
reign, and we'll walk with each oth - er as

live in the free - dom of the cit - y of God.
ha - tred and blind - ness ... will be ... no more.
sis - ters and broth - ers.... u - nit - ed in love.

Refrain

We are called to act with jus-tice, we are called to

love ten - der - ly; we are called to serve one an -

oth - er, to walk hum - bly with God.

Text: David Haas
Music: David Haas

38

Shine, Jesus, shine

Refrain

Shine, Je-sus, shine, fill this land with the Fa-ther's glo-ry;
blaze, Spir-it, blaze, set our hearts on fire.
Flow, riv-er, flow, flood the na-tions with grace and mer-cy;
send forth your Word, Lord, and let there be light!

1 Lord, the light of your love is shin-ing, in the midst of the
2 As we gaze on your king-ly bright-ness, so our fac-es dis-

dark-ness, shin-ing; Je-sus, light of the world, shine up-on us,
play your like-ness, ev-er chang-ing from glo-ry to glo-ry,

set us free by the truth you now bring us.
mir-rored here, may our lives tell your sto-ry.

Refrain

Shine on me, shine on me:

Text: Graham Kendrick
Music: Graham Kendrick

Jesus brings a message

Je-sus brings to the world a spe-cial mes - sage. Ev - 'ry-
Je - sús tra - e u - na no - ti - cia. To - do_el

bo-dy lis-ten up, it's meant for you. There will come a time of peace and of
mun-do se de-be_en - te - rar. Vie-ne_un tiem - po de paz y jus-

jus - tice. Who will help him spread the news? Si-mon, let's go!
ti - cia. ¿Quién le_a - yu - da_a pro - cla - mar? Va-mos, Si - món,

An-drew, you too! Come James and John, to - geth-er we'll march on.
va - mos, An-drés, va - mos, San - tia - go_y Juan . . . tam - bién,

Leave ev - 'ry-thing and fol-low me. Come one, come all, come fol-low me.
de - jen to - do y sí - gan-me, va - mos, . . . sí - gue-me tú tam-bién.

Text: Alejandro Zorzin; tr. William Dexheimer Pharris
Music: Alejandro Zorzin

40

Come to the mountain

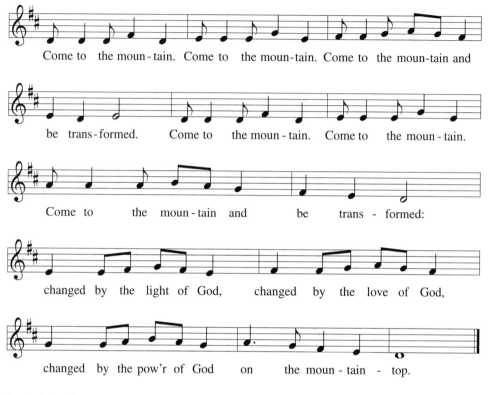

Come to the moun-tain. Come to the moun-tain. Come to the moun-tain and

be trans-formed. Come to the moun - tain. Come to the moun - tain.

Come to the moun - tain and be trans - formed:

changed by the light of God, changed by the love of God,

changed by the pow'r of God on the moun - tain - top.

Text: Pamela L. Hughes
Music: Pamela L. Hughes
© 1995 Living the Good News, Inc.

I want Jesus to walk with me

1   I want Je - sus   to walk with me;
2   In my tri - als,   Lord, walk with me;
3 When I'm in trou - ble,   Lord, walk with me;

I want Je - sus   to walk with me;
in my tri - als,   Lord, walk with me;
when I'm in trou - ble,   Lord, walk with me;

all a - long my pil - grim jour - ney,
when my heart is al - most break - ing,
when my head is bowed in sor - row,

Lord, I want Je - sus to walk with me.
Lord, I want Je - sus to walk with me.
Lord, I want Je - sus to walk with me.

Text: African American spiritual
Music: African American spiritual

42 Is there anybody here who loves my Jesus?

Refrain

Is there an-y-bod-y here who loves my Je - sus,
an-y-bod-y here who loves my Lord? I want to know if you
love my Je - sus; I want to know if you love my Lord.

1 This world's a wil - der - ness of woe,
2 When I was blind and could not see,

Refrain

so let us all to glo - ry go.
King Je - sus brought the light to me.

Text: African American spiritual
Music: African American spiritual

43 Walk in God's ways

1 Walk, walk, walk, walk in God's ways.
2 Jump, jump, jump, jump in God's ways.
3 Hop, hop, hop, hop in God's ways.

Walk, walk, walk, sing - ing God's praise.
Jump, jump, jump, sing - ing God's praise.
Hop, hop, hop, sing - ing God's praise.

Text: Pamela L. Hughes
Music: Pamela L. Hughes
© 1995 Living the Good News, Inc.

Jesus, remember me

44

Je - sus, re - mem-ber me when you come in - to your king - dom.

Je - sus, re - mem-ber me when you come in - to your king - dom.

Text: Luke 23:42
Music: Jacques Berthier
Music © 1981 Les Presses de Taizé, admin. GIA Publications, Inc.

For God so loved the world

45

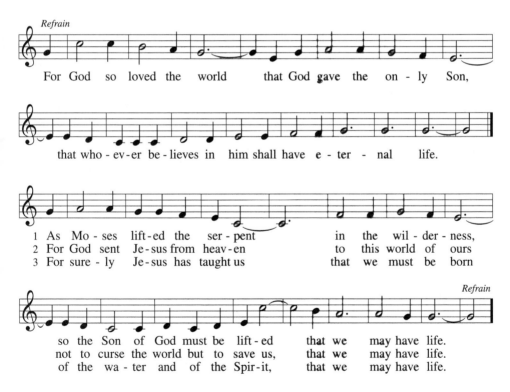

Refrain

For God so loved the world that God gave the on - ly Son,

that who - ev - er be - lieves in him shall have e - ter - nal life.

1 As Mo - ses lift-ed the ser - pent in the wil - der - ness,
2 For God sent Je - sus from heav-en to this world of ours
3 For sure - ly Je - sus has taught us that we must be born

Refrain

so the Son of God must be lift - ed that we may have life.
not to curse the world but to save us, that we may have life.
of the wa - ter and of the Spir - it, that we may have life.

Text: Rusty Edwards
Music: Rusty Edwards
© 1984 Hope Publishing Company

46

Lamb of God

Lamb of God, you take a-way the sin of the world; have

mer-cy on us. Lamb of God, you take a-way the sin of the

world; have mer-cy on us. Lamb of God, you take a-way the

sin of the world; grant us peace.

Text: traditional; tr. International Consultation on English Texts
Music: Richard W. Hillert
Music © 1978 *Lutheran Book of Worship*

Hosanna! the little children sing

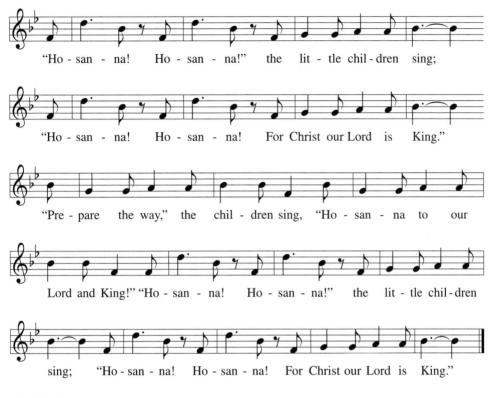

"Ho - san - na! Ho - san - na!" the lit - tle chil - dren sing;

"Ho - san - na! Ho - san - na! For Christ our Lord is King."

"Pre - pare the way," the chil - dren sing, "Ho - san - na to our

Lord and King!" "Ho - san - na! Ho - san - na!" the lit - tle chil - dren

sing; "Ho - san - na! Ho - san - na! For Christ our Lord is King."

Text: Helen Kemp
Music: Helen Kemp
© 1988 Augsburg Fortress

48

All glory, laud, and honor

All glo-ry, laud, and hon - or to you, re-deem-er, king,

to whom the lips of chil - dren made sweet ho-san-nas ring.

1 You are the king of Is - rael and Da-vid's roy - al Son,
2 The com-pa - ny of an - gels is prais-ing you on high;
3 The mul - ti-tude of pil - grims with palms be - fore you went.
4 To you, be-fore your Pas - sion, they sang their hymns of praise.
5 Their prais-es you ac - cept - ed; ac - cept the prayers we bring,

Refrain

now in the Lord's name com - ing, our King and Bless-ed One.
cre - a - tion and all mor - tals in cho-rus make re - ply.
Our praise and prayer and an - thems be - fore you we pre - sent.
To you, now high ex - alt - ed, our mel - o - dy we raise.
great au - thor of all good - ness, O good and gra-cious King.

Text: Theodulph of Orleans; tr. John M. Neale
Music: Melchior Teschner

49

Filled with excitement

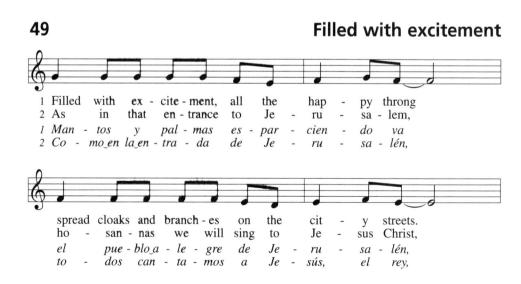

1 Filled with ex - cite - ment, all the hap - py throng
2 As in that en - trance to Je - ru - sa - lem,
1 *Man - tos y pal - mas es - par - cien - do va*
2 *Co - mo en la en - tra - da de Je - ru - sa - lén,*

spread cloaks and branch - es on the cit - y streets.
ho - san - nas we will sing to Je - sus Christ,
el pue - blo_a - le - gre de Je - ru - sa - lén,
to - dos can - ta - mos a Je - sús, el rey,

There in the dis - tance they be - gin to see,
to our re - deem - er who still calls to - day,
a - lláṣa lo le - jos seṣem - pie - zaṣa mi - rar
al Cris - to vi - vo que nos lla - ma hoy

there on a don - key comes the Son of God.
asks us to fol - low with our love and faith.
en un po - lli - no al Hi - jo de Dios.
pa - ra se - guir - le con a - mor y fe.

Refrain

From ev - 'ry cor - ner a thou - sand voic - es sing
Mien - tras, mil vo - ces re - sue - nan por do - quier: Ho -

praise to the one who comes in the name of God.
san - naṣal que vie - neṣen el nom - bre del Se - ñor.

With one great shout of ac - cla - ma - tion loud, tri - um - phant song breaks
Con un a - lien - to de gran ex - cla - ma - ción pro - rrum - pen con voz triun -

forth: Ho - san - na! Ho - san - na to the king!
fal: ¡Ho - san - na! ¡Ho - san - naṣal rey!

Ho - san - na! Ho - san - na to the king!
¡Ho - san - na! ¡Ho - san - naṣal rey!

Text: Rubén Ruiz Avila; tr. Gertrude C. Suppe
Music: Rubén Ruiz Avila

Spanish text and tune © 1972, English trans. © 1979 The United Methodist Publishing House, admin. The Copyright Company

50   Hosanna! This is a special day

1 Ho - san - na!   Ho - san - na!   This   is   a   spe - cial
2 Ho - san - na!   Ho - san - na!   Oh,   how the voic - es

day.   He's com - ing!   He's com - ing!   The   king is   on his   way.
ring.   We   see him!   We   see him!   He   is our King of   kings.

Did   you hear?   Can   it   be?   Rid - ing   on   a   colt   is   he.
Wave the palms,   sing   a   song!   We have wait - ed   for   so   long.

Ho - san - na!   Ho - san - na!   Bless - ed   be   our   Lord.
Ho - san - na!   Ho - san - na!   Bless - ed   be   our   Lord.

Text: Kathleen Donlan Tunseth
Music: Kathleen Donlan Tunseth
© 1995 Kathleen Donlan Tunseth

Were you there

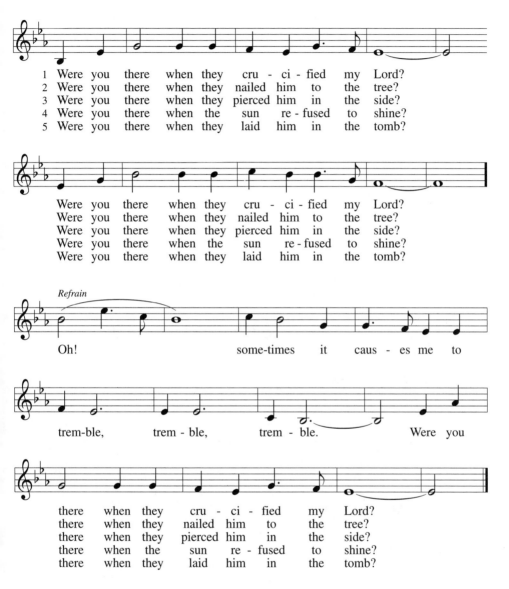

1 Were you there when they cru - ci - fied my Lord?
2 Were you there when they nailed him to the tree?
3 Were you there when they pierced him in the side?
4 Were you there when the sun re - fused to shine?
5 Were you there when they laid him in the tomb?

Were you there when they cru - ci - fied my Lord?
Were you there when they nailed him to the tree?
Were you there when they pierced him in the side?
Were you there when the sun re - fused to shine?
Were you there when they laid him in the tomb?

Refrain

Oh! some-times it caus - es me to

trem-ble, trem - ble, trem - ble. Were you

there when they cru - ci - fied my Lord?
there when they nailed him to the tree?
there when they pierced him in the side?
there when the sun re - fused to shine?
there when they laid him in the tomb?

Text: African American spiritual
Music: African American spiritual

52

Glory be to Jesus

1 Glo - ry be to Je - sus, who, in per - fect love,
2 Glo - ry be to Je - sus, ris - en Lord and king;

died to be my Sav - ior, sent from heav'n a - bove.
on this hap - py Eas - ter al - le - lu - ias sing!

Text: Dorothy N. Schultz
Music: Friedrich Filitz
Text © 1989 CPH Publishing

53

Do you know who died for me?

1 Do you know who died for me? Je - sus did, Je - sus did.
2 Do you know who rose for me? Je - sus did, Je - sus did.
3 Do you know who lives for me? Je - sus does, Je - sus does.
4 Do you know who cares for me? Je - sus does, Je - sus does.

Lov - ing - ly he died for me, yes, he real - ly did!
Lov - ing - ly he rose for me, yes, he real - ly did!
Lov - ing - ly he lives for me, yes, he real - ly does!
Lov - ing - ly he cares for me, yes, he real - ly does!

Text: O. William Luecke
Music: O. William Luecke
© O. William Luecke

This is the feast 54

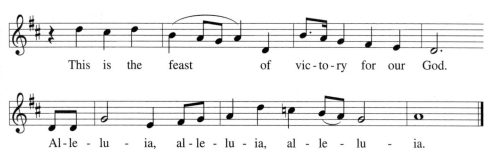

This is the feast of vic-to-ry for our God.

Al-le-lu - ia, al-le-lu-ia, al-le-lu - ia.

Text: John W. Arthur
Music: Richard W. Hillert
Text © 1978 Lutheran Book of Worship
Music © 1978 Richard Hillert, admin. Augsburg Fortress

Now the green blade rises 55

1 Now the green blade ris - es from the bur - ied grain,
2 In the grave they laid him, love by ha - tred slain,
3 Forth he came at Eas - ter, like the ris - en grain,
4 When our hearts are win - try, griev - ing, or in pain,

wheat that in dark earth man - y days has lain;
think - ing that he would nev - er wake a - gain,
he that for three days in the grave had lain;
your touch can call us back to life a - gain,

love lives a - gain, that with the dead has been;
laid in the earth like grain that sleeps un - seen;
raised from the dead my ris - en Lord is seen;
fields of our hearts that dead and bare have been;

love is come a - gain like wheat a - ris - ing green.
love is come a - gain like wheat a - ris - ing green.
love is come a - gain like wheat a - ris - ing green.
love is come a - gain like wheat a - ris - ing green.

Text: John M. C. Crum
Music: French carol
Text © 1928 Oxford University Press

56
In the bulb there is a flower

Hymn of promise

1 In the bulb there is a flow - er; in the seed, an ap-ple tree;
2 There's a song in ev-'ry si - lence, seek-ing word and mel-o - dy;
3 In our end is our be - gin-ning; in our time, in-fin-i - ty;

in co - coons, a hid-den prom-ise: but - ter-flies will soon be free!
there's a dawn in ev - 'ry dark-ness, bring-ing hope to you and me.
in our doubt there is be - liev-ing; in our life, e - ter-ni - ty;

In the cold and snow of win - ter there's a spring that waits to be,
From the past will come the fu - ture; what it holds, a mys-ter - y,
in our death, a res - ur - rec - tion; at the last, a vic-to - ry,

un - re - vealed un - til its sea - son, some-thing God a-lone can see.

Text: Natalie Sleeth
Music: Natalie Sleeth
© 1986 Hope Publishing Company

57
Jesus Christ is risen today

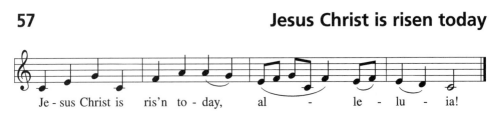

Je - sus Christ is ris'n to - day, al - le - lu - ia!

Text: Latin carol; tr. *Lyra Davidica*
Music: *Lyra Davidica*

Alleluia, alleluia, give thanks

58

Alleluia No. 1

Refrain

Al - le - lu - ia, al - le - lu - ia, give thanks to the ris - en Lord;

al - le - lu - ia, al - le - lu - ia, give praise to his name.

1 Je - sus is Lord of all the earth;
2 Spread the good news o'er all the earth:
3 We have been cru - ci - fied with Christ;
4 Come, let us praise the liv - ing God,

Refrain

he is the king of cre - a - tion.
Je - sus has died and has ris - en.
now we shall live . . . for - ev - er.
joy - ful - ly sing to our Sav - ior.

Text: Donald Fishel
Music: Donald Fishel

59

There's new life in Jesus

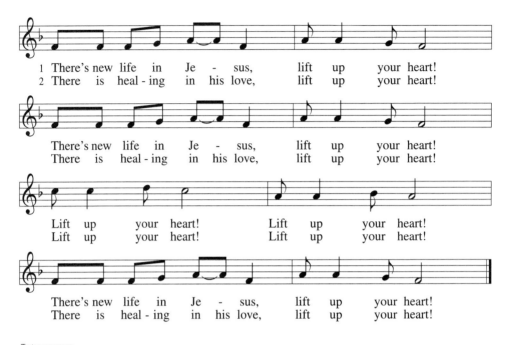

1 There's new life in Je - sus, lift up your heart!
2 There is heal - ing in his love, lift up your heart!

There's new life in Je - sus, lift up your heart!
There is heal - ing in his love, lift up your heart!

Lift up your heart! Lift up your heart!
Lift up your heart! Lift up your heart!

There's new life in Je - sus, lift up your heart!
There is heal - ing in his love, lift up your heart!

Text: anonymous
Music: anonymous

This is the day

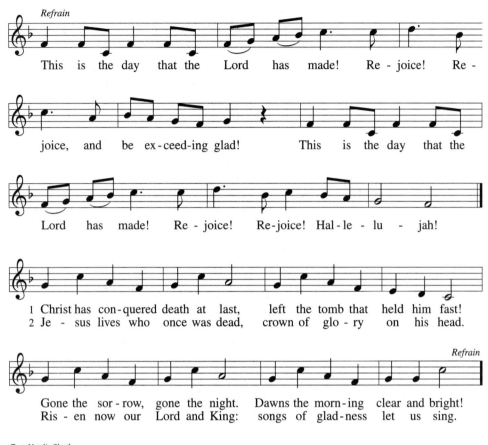

Refrain

This is the day that the Lord has made! Re - joice! Re - joice, and be ex - ceed-ing glad! This is the day that the Lord has made! Re - joice! Re-joice! Hal - le - lu - jah!

1 Christ has con-quered death at last, left the tomb that held him fast!
2 Je - sus lives who once was dead, crown of glo - ry on his head.

Refrain

Gone the sor - row, gone the night. Dawns the morn-ing clear and bright!
Ris - en now our Lord and King: songs of glad-ness let us sing.

Text: Natalie Sleeth
Music: Natalie Sleeth

© 1976 Hinshaw Music, Inc.

61

Come and see

1 The night was dark and filled with gloom.
2 Then sud-den-ly the Lord ap-peared (Come and see! Come and see.)
3 Well, Thom-as said, "My God, my Lord!"

They hid with-in a se-cret room.
to see his friends and calm their fears. (Come and see! Come and see.)
Now I be-lieve the liv-ing Word.

Now Thom-as had not seen the Lord.
To Thom-as he said, "See my hand." (Come and see! Come and see.)
Go tell the peo-ple far and wide,

He doubt-ed ev-'ry sin-gle word.
It hap-pened just as God had planned. (Come and see! Come and see.)
'twas for their sins that Je-sus died.

Refrain

I be-lieve this is Je-sus! Come and see! Come and see. Oh,

I be-lieve this is Je-sus! Come and see! Come and see.

Text: John Ylvisaker, based on John 20:24-28
Music: African American spiritual
Text © 1982 John Ylvisaker

Alleluia! Jesus is risen!

62

1 Al - le - lu - ia! Je - sus is ris - en!
2 Walk - ing the way, Christ in the cen - ter
3 Je - sus the vine, we are the branch - es;
4 Weep-ing, be gone; sor - row, be si - lent:
5 Cit - y of God, Eas - ter for - ev - er,

Trum - pets re - sound - ing in glo - ri - ous light!
tell - ing the sto - ry to o - pen our eyes;
life in the Spir - it the fruit of the tree;
death put a - sun - der, and Eas - ter is bright.
gold - en Je - ru - sa - lem, Je - sus the Lamb,

Splen - dor, the Lamb, heav - en for - ev - er!
break - ing our bread, giv - ing us glo - ry:
heav - en to earth, Christ to the peo - ple,
Cher - u - bim sing: "O grave, be o - pen!"
riv - er of life, saints and arch - an - gels,

Oh, what a mir - a - cle God has in sight!
Je - sus our bless - ing, our con - stant sur - prise.
gift of the fu - ture now flow - ing to me.
Clothe us in won - der, a - dorn us in light.
sing with cre - a - tion to God the I AM!

Refrain

Je - sus is ris - en and we shall a - rise:

Give God the glo - ry! Al - le - lu - ia!

Text: Herbert F. Brokering
Music: David N. Johnson
Text © 1995 Augsburg Fortress
Tune © 1968 Augsburg Publishing House

63 He is Lord

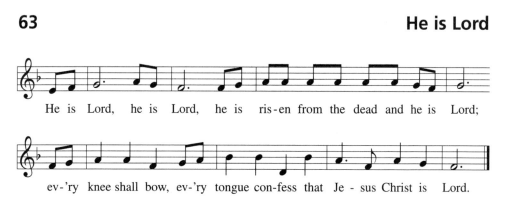

He is Lord, he is Lord, he is ris-en from the dead and he is Lord;

ev-'ry knee shall bow, ev-'ry tongue con-fess that Je - sus Christ is Lord.

Text: Philippians 2:10-11, adapt.
Music: traditional

64 Christ the Lord is risen today!

1 "Christ the Lord is ris'n to - day!" All on earth with an - gels say;
2 Lives a - gain our glo-rious king! Where, O death, is now your sting?

raise your joys and tri - umphs high; sing, ye heav'ns; and earth, re - ply.
Once he died our souls to save; where your vic - to - ry, O grave?

Text: Charles Wesley
Music: French traditional

The Lord is my shepherd

may be sung as a round

Text: Psalm 23:1-2
Music: traditional

66 Gracious Spirit, heed our pleading

1 Gra - cious Spir - it, heed our plead - ing, fash - ion us all a - new.
2 Come to teach us, come to nour - ish those who be - lieve in Christ.
3 Guide our think - ing and our speak - ing done in your ho - ly name.
4 Not mere knowl-edge, but dis - cern - ment, nor root - less lib - er - ty;
5 Keep us fer - vent in our wit - ness; un-swayed by earth's al - lure.

It's your lead - ing that we're need-ing, help us to fol - low you.
Bless the faith - ful, may they flour - ish, strength-ened by grace un - priced.
Mo - ti - vate all in their seek - ing, free - ing from guilt and shame.
turn dis - qui - et to con - tent-ment, doubt in - to cer - tain - ty.
Ev - er grant us zeal-ous fit - ness, which you a - lone as - sure.

Refrain/Kipokeo

Come, come, come, Ho - ly Spir - it, come.
Njo - o, njo - o, njo - o, Ro - ho mwe - ma.

Come, come, come, Ho - ly Spir - it, come.
Njo - o, njo - o, njo - o, Ro - ho mwe - ma.

Text: Wilson Niwagila; tr. Howard S. Olson
Music: Wilson Niwagila

Come, O Holy Spirit, come

67

All
Come, O   Ho-ly Spir-it, come,
Wa   wa   wa   E - mi - mi - mo,

Leader
Ho-ly Spir-it, come.
E - mi - o - lo - ye.

All
Come, al - might-y Spir-it,
Wa   wa   wa   A - lag - ba -

Leader
come,
ra,
al-might-y Spir-it, come.
A - lag - ba - ra - me - ta.

All
Come,   come,
Wa - o   wa - o

Leader
come.
wa - o.
O Spir-it, come.
E - mi - mi - mo.

Text and music: The Church of the Lord (Aladura); transc. and para. I-to Loh

68

Spirit, Spirit of gentleness

Refrain

Spir - it, Spir-it of gen-tle-ness, blow through the wil-der-ness

call-ing and free; Spir - it, Spir-it of rest-less-ness,

stir me from plac-id-ness, wind, wind on the sea.

1 You moved on the wa - ters, you called to the
2 You swept through the des - ert, you stung with the
3 You sang in a sta - ble, you cried from a
4 You call from to - mor - row, you break an - cient

deep, then you coaxed up the moun - tains from the
sand and you goad - ed your peo - ple with a
hill, then you whis - pered in si - lence when the
schemes. From the bond - age of sor - row all the

val - leys of sleep; and o - ver the e -
law and a land; and when they were blind -
whole world was still; and down in the cit -
cap - tives dream dreams; our wom - en see vi -

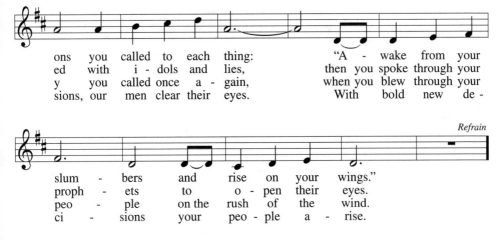

ons   you   called to   each   thing: "A - wake from your
ed   with i - dols and   lies,   then you spoke through your
y   you   called once a - gain,   when you blew through your
sions, our   men   clear their eyes.   With   bold   new   de -

Refrain

slum - bers   and   rise   on   your   wings."
proph - ets   to   o - pen their   eyes.
peo   - ple   on the rush   of   the   wind.
ci   - sions   your   peo - ple a - rise.

Text: James K. Manley
Music: James K. Manley
© 1978 James K. Manley

69

Spirit Friend

1 God sends us the Spir - it to be - friend and help us,
2 Dark-ened roads are clear - er, heav - y bur - dens light - er,
3 Now we are God's peo - ple, bond - ed by God's pres - ence,

re - cre - ate and guide us, Spir - it Friend.
when we're walk - ing with our Spir - it Friend.
a - gents of God's pur - pose, Spir - it Friend.

Spir - it who en - liv - ens, sanc - ti - fies, en - light - ens,
Now we need not fear the pow - ers of the dark - ness.
Lead us for - ward ev - er, slip - ping back-ward nev - er,

sets us free, is now our Spir - it Friend.
None can o - ver - come our Spir - it Friend.
to your re - made world, our Spir - it Friend.

Refrain

Spir-it of our mak - er, Spir-it Friend. Spir - it of our Je - su,

Spir-it Friend. Spir - it of God's peo - ple, Spir - it Friend.

*hand claps

Text: Tom Colvin
Music: Gonja traditional, adapt. Tom Colvin
© 1987 Hope Publishing Company

Holy, Holy Spirit

Refrain

Ho - ly, Ho - ly Spir - it, ho - ly, ho - ly dove, ho - ly, ho - ly help - er, ho - ly fire of love, ho - ly fire of love.

1 In a room his fol - l'wers wait - ed,
2 Then a rush - ing wind came blow - ing,
3 Then they spoke, and all who lis - tened
4 Break our qui - et, fear - ful si - lence

sad - dened by their Sav - ior's loss. It was ear - ly
and they saw the flames a - glow. Then they felt the
heard the gos - pel sto - ry told. Then three thou - sand
with the Spir - it's wind and fire. Flame our hearts to

Refrain

in the morn - ing on the day called Pen - te - cost.
Spir - it's pow - er rest - ing on their heads be - low.
strong were bap - tized and the church of Christ was born!
great - er ser - vice; mold our faith as you de - sire.

Text: Scott Tunseth
Music: Kathleen Donlan Tunseth
Text © 1996 Scott Tunseth
Music © 1996 Kathleen Donlan Tunseth

71

O day full of grace

1 O day full of grace that now we see ap - pear - ing on
2 God came to us then at Pen - te - cost, his Spir - it new
3 When we on that fi - nal jour - ney go that Christ is for

earth's ho - ri - zon, bring light from our God that we may
life re - veal - ing, that we might no more from him be
us pre - par - ing, we'll gath - er in song, our hearts a -

be re - plete in his joy this sea - son. God, shine for us
lost, all dark - ness for us dis - pel - ling. His flame will the
glow, all joy of . . . heav - ens shar - ing, and walk in the

now in this dark place; your name on our hearts em - bla - zon.
mark of sin ef - face and bring to us all his heal - ing.
light of God's own place, with an - gels his name a - dor - ing.

Text: Danish folk hymn; tr. Gerald Thorson
Music: Christoph E. F. Weyse
Tr. © 1978 *Lutheran Book of Worship*

Spirit of the living God

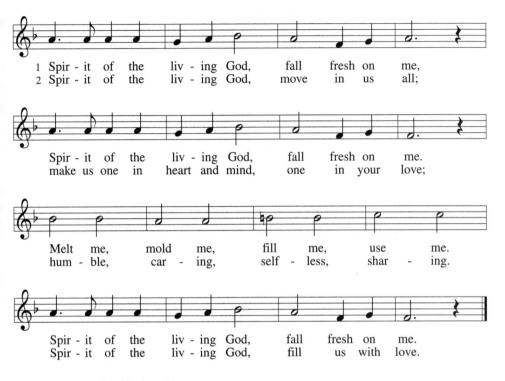

1 Spir - it of the liv - ing God, fall fresh on me,
2 Spir - it of the liv - ing God, move in us all;

Spir - it of the liv - ing God, fall fresh on me.
make us one in heart and mind, one in your love;

Melt me, mold me, fill me, use me.
hum - ble, car - ing, self - less, shar - ing.

Spir - it of the liv - ing God, fall fresh on me.
Spir - it of the liv - ing God, fill us with love.

Text: Daniel Iverson, st.1; Michael Baughen, st. 2
Music: Daniel Iverson

73

Come! Come! Everybody worship

Refrain

Come! Come! Ev'ry-bod-y wor-ship with a prayer or song of praise!
¡Ven - gan to-dos a-do-re-mos con can-tos y o - ra-ción!

Come! Come! Ev'ry-bod-y wor-ship! Wor-ship God al-ways!
¡Ven - gan to-dos a-do-re-mos a nues-tro Se - ñor!

1 Wor-ship and re - mem-ber to keep the Sab-bath day.
2 Wor-ship and re - mem-ber the Lord's un-end-ing care,
3 Wor-ship and re - mem-ber your bless-ings great and small.
4 Wor-ship and re - mem-ber how Je - sus long a - go
5 Wor-ship and re - mem-ber that God is like a light:

Refrain

Take a rest and think of God; put your work a - way.
reach-ing out to love and help peo - ple ev - 'ry - where.
Give to God an of - fer - ing; show your thanks for all.
taught us how to talk to God; some-thing we should know.
show-ing you the way to go, ev - er burn-ing bright!

Text: Natalie Sleeth; tr. Mary Lou Santillán-Baert
Music: Natalie Sleeth

Come and sing your praise
74

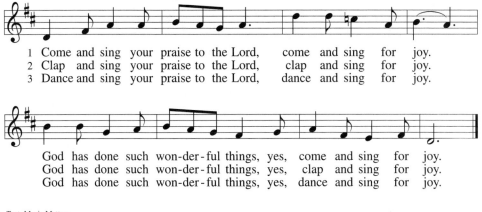

1 Come and sing your praise to the Lord, come and sing for joy.
2 Clap and sing your praise to the Lord, clap and sing for joy.
3 Dance and sing your praise to the Lord, dance and sing for joy.

God has done such won-der-ful things, yes, come and sing for joy.
God has done such won-der-ful things, yes, clap and sing for joy.
God has done such won-der-ful things, yes, dance and sing for joy.

Text: Music Matters
Music: Catherine Mathia
© 1995 Music Matters

Come and sing together
75

1 Come and sing to-geth-er, come and sing to-geth-er,
2 Sing hel-lo to *name*, sing hel-lo to *name*,
3 Go well and go safe-ly, go well and go safe-ly,

come and sing to-geth-er. We've come to praise the Lord.
sing hel-lo to *name*. We've come to praise the Lord.
go well and go safe-ly. The Lord be ev-er with you.

Text: Music Matters
Music: traditional
Text © 1995 Music Matters

76

Hello, everybody

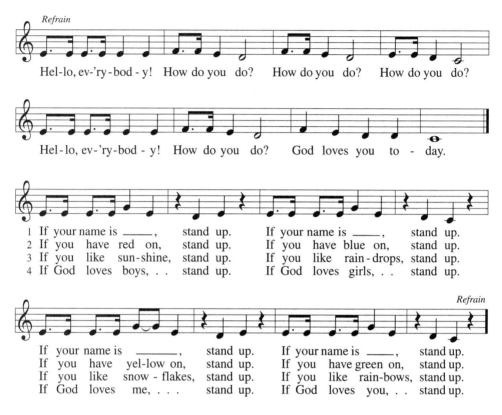

Refrain

Hel-lo, ev-'ry-bod - y! How do you do? How do you do? How do you do?

Hel-lo, ev-'ry-bod - y! How do you do? God loves you to - day.

1 If your name is _____, stand up.   If your name is _____, stand up.
2 If you have red on, stand up.   If you have blue on, stand up.
3 If you like sun-shine, stand up.   If you like rain-drops, stand up.
4 If God loves boys, . . stand up.   If God loves girls, . . stand up.

Refrain

If your name is _____, stand up.   If your name is _____, stand up.
If you have yel-low on, stand up.   If you have green on, stand up.
If you like snow - flakes, stand up.   If you like rain-bows, stand up.
If God loves me, . . . stand up.   If God loves you, . . stand up.

Text: traditional
Music: traditional

Come into God's presence 77

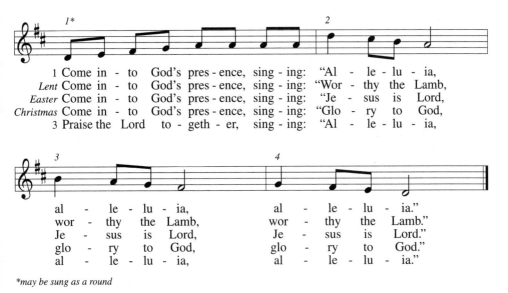

1 Come in - to God's pres - ence, sing - ing: "Al - le - lu - ia,
Lent Come in - to God's pres - ence, sing - ing: "Wor - thy the Lamb,
Easter Come in - to God's pres - ence, sing - ing: "Je - sus is Lord,
Christmas Come in - to God's pres - ence, sing - ing: "Glo - ry to God,
3 Praise the Lord to - geth - er, sing - ing: "Al - le - lu - ia,

al - le - lu - ia, al - le - lu - ia."
wor - thy the Lamb, wor - thy the Lamb."
Je - sus is Lord, Je - sus is Lord."
glo - ry to God, glo - ry to God."
al - le - lu - ia, al - le - lu - ia."

may be sung as a round

Text: Music Matters
Music: Russian folk song
Text © 1995 Music Matters

Won't you come and sit with me 78

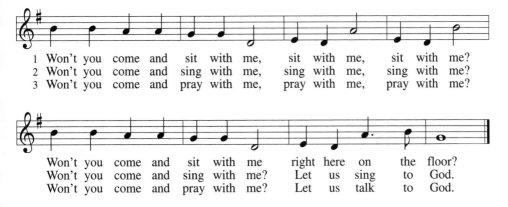

1 Won't you come and sit with me, sit with me, sit with me?
2 Won't you come and sing with me, sing with me, sing with me?
3 Won't you come and pray with me, pray with me, pray with me?

Won't you come and sit with me right here on the floor?
Won't you come and sing with me? Let us sing to God.
Won't you come and pray with me? Let us talk to God.

Text: anonymous, st. 1; Jane Haas, sts. 2-3
Music: anonymous

79

Listen, God is calling

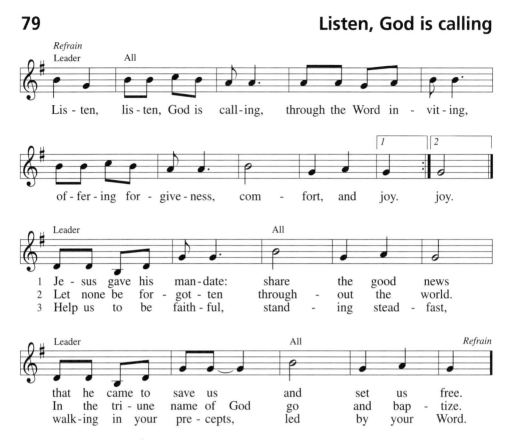

Refrain

Leader   All

Lis - ten,   lis - ten, God is   call-ing,   through the Word in - vit-ing,

of - fer - ing for - give-ness,   com - fort, and   joy.   joy.

Leader   All

1 Je - sus gave his   man-date: share   the   good   news
2 Let none be   for - got - ten   through - out   the   world.
3 Help us   to   be   faith - ful,   stand - ing   stead - fast,

Leader   All   *Refrain*

that   he   came to   save   us   and   set   us   free.
In   the   tri - une   name of   God   go   and   bap - tize.
walk-ing   in   your   pre - cepts,   led   by   your   Word.

Text: Tanzanian traditional; tr. Howard S. Olson
Music: Tanzanian tune
Tr. © Lutheran Theological College, admin. Augsburg Fortress

How firm a foundation

80

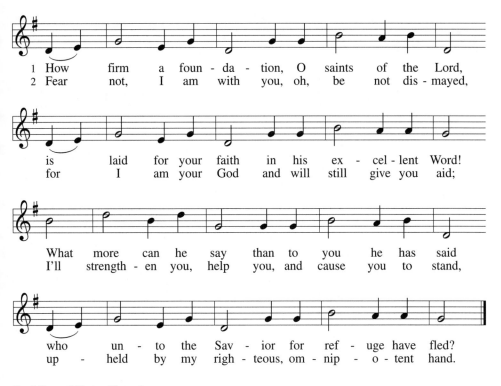

1 How firm a foun - da - tion, O saints of the Lord,
2 Fear not, I am with you, oh, be not dis - mayed,

is laid for your faith in his ex - cel - lent Word!
for I am your God and will still give you aid;

What more can he say than to you he has said
I'll strength - en you, help you, and cause you to stand,

who un - to the Sav - ior for ref - uge have fled?
up - held by my righ - teous, om - nip - o - tent hand.

Text: J. Rippon, *A Selection of Hymns*, alt.
Music: North American traditional

81   A mighty fortress is our God

1 A might-y for-tress is our God, a sword and shield vic-
2 No strength of ours can match his might! We would be lost, re-
3 Though hordes of dev-ils fill the land all threat-'ning to de-
4 God's Word for-ev-er shall a-bide, no thanks to foes, who

to - rious; he breaks the cruel op-pres-sor's rod and
ject - ed. But now a cham-pion comes to fight, whom
vour us, we trem-ble not, un-moved we stand; they
fear it; for God him-self fights by our side with

wins sal-va-tion glo - rious. The old sa-tan-ic foe
God him-self e - lect - ed. You ask who this may be?
can-not o-ver-pow'r us. Let this world's ty-rant rage;
weap-ons of the Spir - it. Were they to take our house,

has sworn to work us woe! With craft and dread-ful might
The Lord of hosts is he! Christ Je-sus, might-y Lord,
in bat-tle we'll en-gage! His might is doomed to fail;
goods, hon-or, child, or spouse, though life be wrenched a-way,

he arms him-self to fight. On earth he has no e - qual.
God's on-ly Son, a-dored. He holds the field vic-to - rious.
God's judg-ment must pre-vail! One lit-tle word sub-dues him.
they can-not win the day. The king-dom's ours for-ev - er!

Text: Martin Luther; tr. *Lutheran Book of Worship*
Music: Martin Luther
Tr. © 1978 *Lutheran Book of Worship*

Alleluia. Lord, to whom shall we go?

Al - le - lu - ia. Lord, to whom shall we go? You have the

words of e - ter - nal life. Al - le - lu - ia, al - le - lu - ia.

Text: John 6:68, adapt. *Lutheran Book of Worship*
Music: Richard W. Hillert
© 1978 *Lutheran Book of Worship*

Lord, let my heart be good soil   83

Lord, let my heart be good soil, o - pen to the seed of your

word. Lord, let my heart be good soil, where

love can grow and peace is un - der - stood. When my heart is hard,

break the stone a - way. When my heart is cold, warm it with the day.

When my heart is lost, lead me on your way. Lord, let my heart,

Lord, let my heart, Lord, let my heart be good soil.

Text: Handt Hanson
Music: Handt Hanson

© 1985 Prince of Peace Publishing, Changing Church, Inc.

84 Open your ears, O faithful people

1 O - pen your ears, O faith - ful peo - ple,
2 They who have ears to hear the mes - sage,
3 Is - ra - el comes to greet the Sav - ior,

o - pen your ears and hear God's Word. O - pen your hearts, O
they who have ears, now let them hear; they who would learn the
Ju - dah is glad to see his day, from east and west the

roy - al priest - hood, God has come to you.
way of wis - dom, let them hear God's Word.
peo - ples trav - el, God will show the way.

Refrain

God has spo - ken to the peo - ple, hal - le - lu - jah!
To - rah o - ra, To - rah o - ra, hal - le - lu - jah!

God has spo - ken words of wis - dom, hal - le - lu - jah!
To - rah o - ra, To - rah o - ra, hal - le - lu - jah!

God has spo - ken to the peo - ple, hal - le - lu - jah!
To - rah o - ra, To - rah o - ra, hal - le - lu - jah!

God has spo - ken words of wis - dom, hal - le - lu - jah!
To - rah o - ra, To - rah o - ra, hal - le - lu - jah!

Text: Hasidic traditional; English text, Willard F. Jabusch
Music: Hasidic tune

You have put on Christ 85

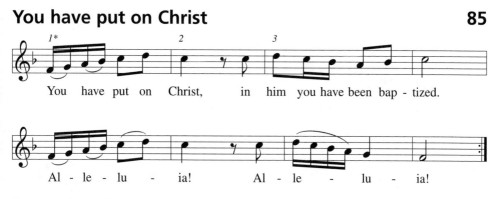

You have put on Christ, in him you have been bap - tized.

Al - le - lu - ia! Al - le - lu - ia!

*may be sung as a round

Text: Galatians 3:27, adapt. International Commission on English in the Liturgy
Music: Howard Hughes
Text © 1969 ICEL
Music © 1977 ICEL

I was baptized, happy day! 86

I was bap - tized, hap - py day! All my sins were washed a - way.

God looked down on me and smiled. I be - came God's own dear child.

Text: Arnold Mueller
Music: French traditional
Text © 1949 CPH Publishing

87

Baptized in water

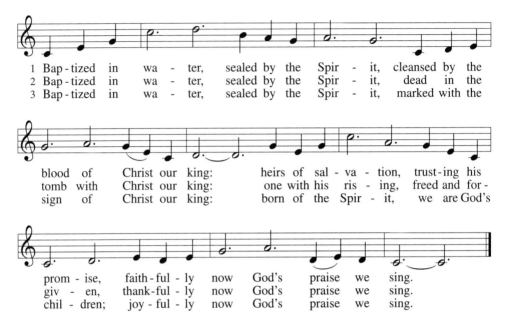

1 Bap - tized in wa - ter, sealed by the Spir - it, cleansed by the
2 Bap - tized in wa - ter, sealed by the Spir - it, dead in the
3 Bap - tized in wa - ter, sealed by the Spir - it, marked with the

blood of Christ our king: heirs of sal - va - tion, trust-ing his
tomb with Christ our king: one with his ris - ing, freed and for -
sign of Christ our king: born of the Spir - it, we are God's

prom - ise, faith - ful - ly now God's praise we sing.
giv - en, thank-ful - ly now God's praise we sing.
chil - dren; joy - ful - ly now God's praise we sing.

Text: Michael Saward
Music: Gaelic traditional
Text © 1982 Hope Publishing Company

Lift high the cross

88

Refrain

Lift high the cross, the love of Christ pro-claim till

all the world a-dore his sa-cred name.

1 Come, Chris-tians, fol-low where our cap-tain trod,
2 Led on their way by this tri-um-phant sign,
3 All new-born sol-diers of the Cru-ci-fied
4 O Lord, once lift-ed on the glo-rious tree,
5 So shall our song of tri-umph ev-er be:

Refrain

our king vic-to-rious, Christ, the Son of God.
the hosts of God in con-qu'ring ranks com-bine.
bear on their brows the seal of him who died.
as thou hast prom-ised, draw us all to thee.
praise to the Cru-ci-fied for vic-to-ry!

Text: George W. Kitchin and Michael R. Newbolt
Music: Sydney H. Nicholson
© 1974 Hope Publishing Company

89   I've just come from the fountain

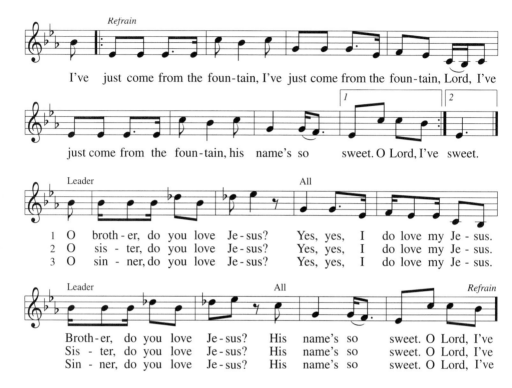

Refrain

I've just come from the foun-tain, I've just come from the foun-tain, Lord, I've

just come from the foun-tain, his name's so sweet. O Lord, I've sweet.

Leader   All

1 O broth-er, do you love Je-sus? Yes, yes, I do love my Je-sus.
2 O sis-ter, do you love Je-sus? Yes, yes, I do love my Je-sus.
3 O sin-ner, do you love Je-sus? Yes, yes, I do love my Je-sus.

Leader   All   *Refrain*

Broth-er, do you love Je-sus? His name's so sweet. O Lord, I've
Sis-ter, do you love Je-sus? His name's so sweet. O Lord, I've
Sin-ner, do you love Je-sus? His name's so sweet. O Lord, I've

Text: African American spiritual
Music: African American spiritual

Seek ye first

1 Seek ye first the king - dom of God and its
2 Ask and it shall be giv - en un - to you; seek and

righ - teous - ness, and all these things shall be
you shall find; knock and the door shall be

add - ed un - to you. Al - le - lu, al - le - lu - ia.
o - pened un - to you. Al - le - lu, al - le - lu - ia.

Text: Matt. 6:33, 7:7, adapt. Karen Lafferty
Music: Karen Lafferty

91
Every time I feel the spirit

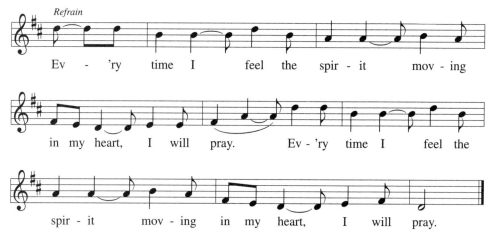

Ev - 'ry time I feel the spir - it mov - ing
in my heart, I will pray. Ev - 'ry time I feel the
spir - it mov - ing in my heart, I will pray.

Text: African American spiritual
Music: African American spiritual

92
Jesus listens when I pray

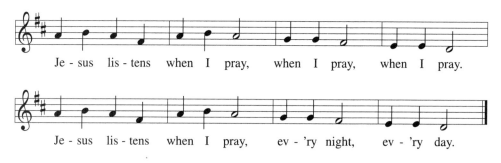

Je - sus lis - tens when I pray, when I pray, when I pray.
Je - sus lis - tens when I pray, ev - 'ry night, ev - 'ry day.

Text: Clara Ketelhut
Music: Arthur W. Gross
© 1960 CPH Publishing

It's me, O Lord

Refrain

It's me, it's me, O Lord, stand-in' in the need of prayer;

it's me, it's me, O Lord, stand-in' in the need of prayer.

1 Not my broth - er, not my sis - ter, but it's me, O Lord,
2 Not the preach - er, not the dea - con, but it's me, O Lord,
3 Not my fa - ther, not my moth - er, but it's me, O Lord,
4 Not the strang - er, not my neigh-bor, but it's me, O Lord,

stand-in' in the need of prayer; not my broth - er, not my sis - ter, but it's
stand-in' in the need of prayer; not the preach-er, not the dea - con, but it's
stand-in' in the need of prayer; not my fa - ther, not my moth-er, but it's
stand-in' in the need of prayer; not the strang - er, not my neigh-bor, but it's

Refrain

me, O Lord, stand-in' in the need of prayer.
me, O Lord, stand-in' in the need of prayer.
me, O Lord, stand-in' in the need of prayer.
me, O Lord, stand-in' in the need of prayer.

Text: African American spiritual
Music: African American spiritual

94   Lord, listen to your children praying

Lord, lis-ten to your chil-dren pray-ing, Lord, send your Spir-it in this place;

Lord, lis-ten to your chil-dren pray-ing, send us love, send us pow'r, send us grace.

Text: Ken Medema
Music: Ken Medema
© 1973 Hope Publishing Company

95   Let my prayer rise

Let my prayer rise be - fore you as in - cense; the

lift - ing up of my hands as the eve - ning sac - ri - fice.

Text: Psalm 141:2, adapt. *Lutheran Book of Worship*
Music: David Schack
© 1978 *Lutheran Book of Worship*

Our Father in heaven

Our Fa - ther in heav - en, hal - lowed be your name,

your king - dom come, your will be done,

On earth as in heav - en. Give us to - day our

dai - ly bread. For - give us our sins as

we for - give those who sin a - gainst us. Save us from the

time of tri - al and de - liv - er us from e - vil.

For the king - dom, the pow'r, and the glo - ry are

yours, now and for - ev - er. A - men

Text: Lord's Prayer, tr. International Consultation on English Texts
Music: plainsong

97

Come, Lord Jesus

1 Oh, come, Lord Je - sus, be our guest, and
2 Oh, come, Lord Je - sus, be our guest, and
3 Oh, come, Lord Je - sus, be our guest, and
4 Oh, come, Lord Je - sus, be our guest, and

let your gifts to us be blest. Keep us for - ev - er
let your gifts to us be blest. Oh, may there be a
let your gifts to us be blest. Guide us a - long the
let your gifts to us be blest. Come deep with - in our

in your sight, and be our joy, our hearts' de - light.
good - ly share on ev - 'ry ta - ble ev - 'ry - where.
ser - vant's way, and lead us to your dawn - ing day.
hearts to dwell, that we may all your good - ness tell.

Text: traditional table prayer, adapt. Susan Briehl
Music: Thomas Tallis
Text © 1996 Augsburg Fortress

98

God gave to me a life to live

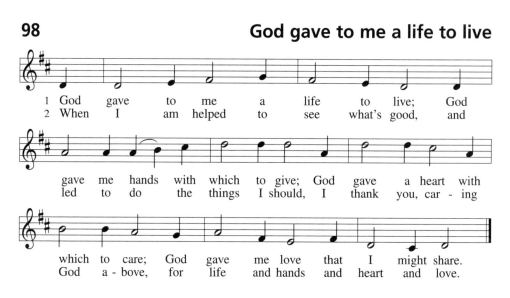

1 God gave to me a life to live; God
2 When I am helped to see what's good, and

gave me hands with which to give; God gave a heart with
led to do the things I should, I thank you, car - ing

which to care; God gave me love that I might share.
God a - bove, for life and hands and heart and love.

Text: anonymous
Music: European tune, adapt. Michael Praetorius

The Lord is good to me

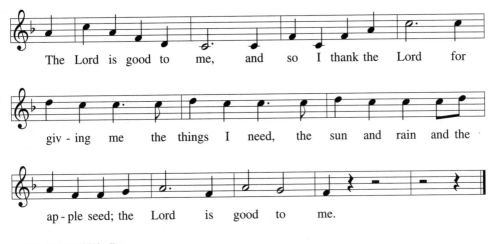

The Lord is good to me, and so I thank the Lord for

giv-ing me the things I need, the sun and rain and the

ap-ple seed; the Lord is good to me.

Text: Kim Gannon and Walter Kent
Music: Kim Gannon and Walter Kent
© 1946 Walt Disney Music Company

100

Let the vineyards be fruitful

Let the vine-yards be fruit-ful, Lord, and fill to the brim our cup of

bless-ing. Gath-er a har-vest from the seeds that were sown, that

we may be fed with the bread of life. Gath-er the hopes and

dreams of all; u - nite them with the prayers we of - fer.

Grace our ta-ble with your pres-ence, and give us a fore-taste of the feast to come.

Text: John W. Arthur
Music: Ronald A. Nelson
© 1978 *Lutheran Book of Worship*

I am thanking Jesus   101

English — I am thank-ing Je - sus, I am thank-ing Je - sus, I am thank-ing
Swahili — A - san - te sa - na Ye - su, a - san - te sa - na Ye - su, a - san - te sa - na
Otji-vambo — Tan - di tan - ga Ye - sus, tan - di tan - ga Ye - sus, tan - di tan - ga

Je - sus from my heart. I am thank - ing Je - sus,
Ye - su mo - yo - ni. A - san - te sa - na Ye - su, a -
Ye - sus mo - mu - ti - ma. Tan - di tan - ga Ye - sus,

I am thank-ing Je - sus, I am thank-ing Je - sus from my heart.
san - te sa - na Ye - su, a - san - te sa - na Ye - su mo - yo - ni.
tan - di tan - ga Ye - sus, tan - di tan - ga Ye - sus mo - mu - ti - ma.

Text: Namibian and Tanzanian traditional
Music: African traditional
Tr. © 1986 Augsburg Fortress

All good gifts around us   102

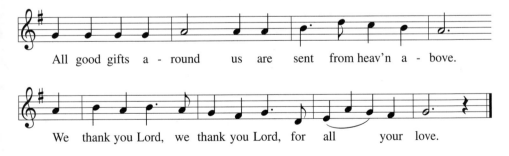

All good gifts a - round us are sent from heav'n a - bove.

We thank you Lord, we thank you Lord, for all your love.

Text: Matthias Claudius; tr. Jane M. Campbell
Music: Johann A. P. Schulz

103

Come, let us eat

1 Come, let us eat, for now the feast is spread,
2 Come, let us drink, for now the wine is poured,
3 In . . . . his pres - ence now we meet and rest,
4 Rise, then, to spread a - broad God's might - y word,

come, let us eat, for now the feast is spread.
come, let us drink, for now the wine is poured.
in . . . . his pres - ence now we meet and rest.
rise, then, to spread a - broad God's might - y word.

Our Lord's bod - y let us take to - geth - er,
Je - sus' blood poured let us drink to - geth - er,
In the pres - ence of our Lord we gath - er,
Je - sus ris - en will bring in the king - dom,

our Lord's bod - y let us take to - geth - er.
Je - sus' blood poured let us drink to - geth - er.
in the pres - ence of our Lord we gath - er.
Je - sus ris - en will bring in the king - dom.

Text: Billema Kwillia, sts. 1-3; Gilbert E. Doan, st. 4, alt.; tr. Margaret D. Miller, sts. 1-3, alt.
Music: Billema Kwillia; arr. Leland Sateren
Text sts. 1-3 and tune © Lutheran World Federation; text st. 4 and arr. © 1972 *Contemporary Worship 4*, admin. Augsburg Fortress

Feed us, Jesus

104

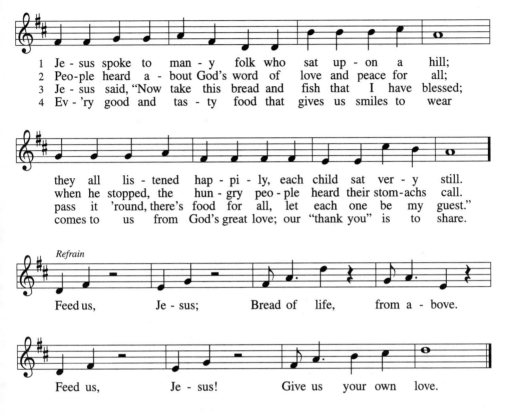

1 Je - sus spoke to man - y folk who sat up - on a hill;
2 Peo - ple heard a - bout God's word of love and peace for all;
3 Je - sus said, "Now take this bread and fish that I have blessed;
4 Ev - 'ry good and tas - ty food that gives us smiles to wear

they all lis - tened hap - pi - ly, each child sat ver - y still.
when he stopped, the hun - gry peo - ple heard their stom - achs call.
pass it 'round, there's food for all, let each one be my guest."
comes to us from God's great love; our "thank you" is to share.

Refrain

Feed us, Je - sus; Bread of life, from a - bove.

Feed us, Je - sus! Give us your own love.

Text: John Folkening
Music: John Folkening
© 1986 Augsburg Fortress

105   I received the living God

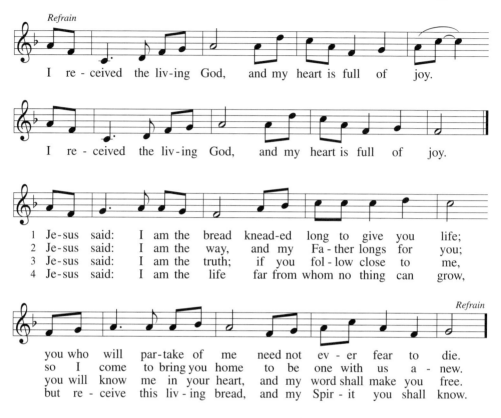

Refrain

I re-ceived the liv-ing God, and my heart is full of joy.

I re-ceived the liv-ing God, and my heart is full of joy.

1 Je-sus said: I am the bread knead-ed long to give you life;
2 Je-sus said: I am the way, and my Fa-ther longs for you;
3 Je-sus said: I am the truth; if you fol-low close to me,
4 Je-sus said: I am the life far from whom no thing can grow,

Refrain

you who will par-take of me need not ev-er fear to die.
so I come to bring you home to be one with us a-new.
you will know me in your heart, and my word shall make you free.
but re-ceive this liv-ing bread, and my Spir-it you shall know.

Text: anonymous
Music: anonymous

To the banquet, come 106

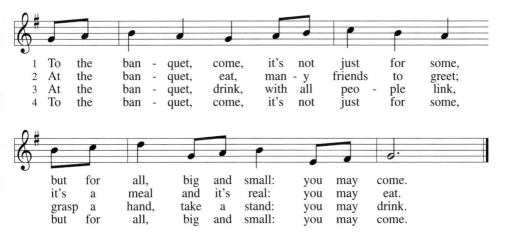

1 To the ban - quet, come, it's not just for some,
2 At the ban - quet, eat, man - y friends to greet;
3 At the ban - quet, drink, with all peo - ple link,
4 To the ban - quet, come, it's not just for some,

but for all, big and small: you may come.
it's a meal and it's real: you may eat.
grasp a hand, take a stand: you may drink.
but for all, big and small: you may come.

Text: Wayne L. Wold
Music: Wayne L. Wold
© 1999 Augsburg Fortress

Shalom 107

Sha - lom, my friends, sha - lom, my friends, sha - lom, sha - lom.
Sha - lom, cha-ve - rim, sha - lom, cha-ve - rim, sha - lom, sha - lom.

Sha - lom my friends, sha - lom, my friends. Sha - lom, sha - lom.
Sha - lom cha-ve-rim, sha - lom cha-ve-rim. Sha - lom, sha - lom.

*may be sung as a round

Text: traditional
Music: Israeli traditional

108

Go now in peace

Go now in peace, go now in peace; may the love of God sur - round you ev - 'ry - where, ev - 'ry - where you may go.

*may be sung as a round

Text: Natalie Sleeth
Music: Natalie Sleeth
© 1976 Hinshaw Music, Inc.

The trees of the field

109

You shall go out with joy and be led forth with peace,

and the moun-tains and the hills will break forth be - fore you.

There'll be shouts of joy and all the trees of the field

will clap, will clap their hands.

And all the trees of the field will clap their hands.

The trees of the field will clap their hands.

The trees of the field will clap their hands,

while you go out with joy.

Text: Steffi Geiser Rubin
Music: Stuart Dauermann

110

Go into the world

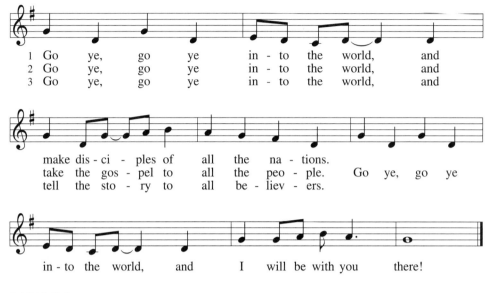

1 Go ye, go ye in-to the world, and
2 Go ye, go ye in-to the world, and
3 Go ye, go ye in-to the world, and

make dis-ci-ples of all the na-tions.
take the gos-pel to all the peo-ple. Go ye, go ye
tell the sto-ry to all be-liev-ers.

in-to the world, and I will be with you there!

Text: Natalie Sleeth
Music: Natalie Sleeth
© 1979 Choristers Guild

Go in peace and serve the Lord

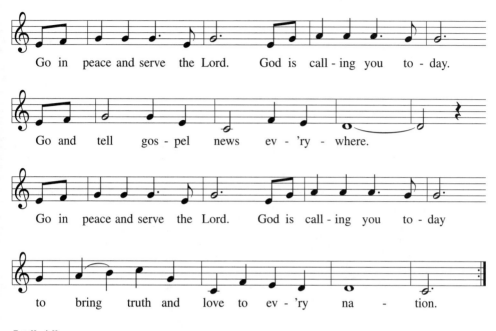

Go in peace and serve the Lord. God is call-ing you to-day.

Go and tell gos-pel news ev-'ry-where.

Go in peace and serve the Lord. God is call-ing you to-day

to bring truth and love to ev-'ry na - tion.

Text: Handt Hanson
Music: Handt Hanson

112

God be with you

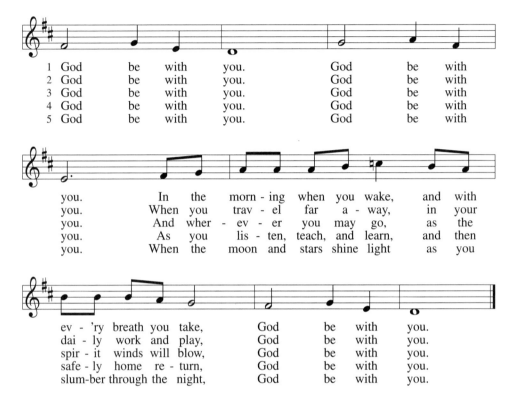

1 God be with you. God be with
2 God be with you. God be with
3 God be with you. God be with
4 God be with you. God be with
5 God be with you. God be with

you. In the morn - ing when you wake, and with
you. When you trav - el far a - way, in your
you. And wher - ev - er you may go, as the
you. As you lis - ten, teach, and learn, and then
you. When the moon and stars shine light as you

ev - 'ry breath you take, God be with you.
dai - ly work and play, God be with you.
spir - it winds will blow, God be with you.
safe - ly home re - turn, God be with you.
slum-ber through the night, God be with you.

Text: Rusty Edwards
Music: Rusty Edwards

The Lord is great!   **113**

Psalm 8

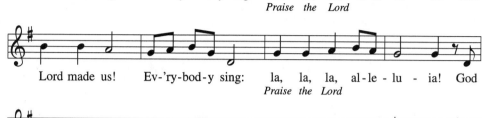

The Lord is great! Ev-'ry-bod-y sing: la, la, la, al-le-lu-ia! The
Praise the Lord

Lord made us! Ev-'ry-bod-y sing: la, la, la, al-le-lu-ia! God
Praise the Lord

made the beasts, the birds in the tree, the fish in the wat-er, and God made me! The

Lord is great! Ev-'ry-bod-y sing: la, la, la, al-le-lu-ia! The
Praise the Lord

Lord is great! Ev-'ry-bod-y sing: la, la, la, al-le-lu-ia!
Praise the Lord

Text: John Erickson
Music: John Erickson

© 1975 Graded Press, admin. The Copyright Company

114

The butterfly song

1 If I were a but-ter - fly, I'd thank you, Lord, for
2 If I were an el - e - phant, I'd thank you, Lord, by
3 If I were a wig-gly worm, I'd thank you, Lord, that

giv-ing me wings. And if I were a rob-in in a tree, I'd
rais-ing my trunk. And if I were a kan - ga - roo, you
I . . . could squirm. And if I were a croc - o - dile, I'd

thank you, Lord, that I could sing. And if I were a
know I'd hop right up to you. And if I were an
thank you, Lord, for my big smile. And if I were a

fish in the sea, I'd wig-gle my tail and I'd gig-gle with glee. But
oc - to - pus, I'd thank you, Lord, for . . . my . . . fine looks. But
fuz-zy-wuz-zy bear, I'd thank you, Lord, for my fuz-zy-wuz-zy hair. But

I just thank you, Fa-ther, for mak-ing me me.
I just thank you, Fa-ther, for mak-ing me me.
I just thank you, Fa-ther, for mak-ing me me.

Refrain

For you gave me a heart and you gave me a smile. You

gave me Je-sus and you made me your child. And I just thank you,

Fa - ther, for mak - ing me me.

Text: Brian Howard
Music: Brian Howard
© 1974 Mission Hills Music, admin. The Copyright Company

You made every part of me 115

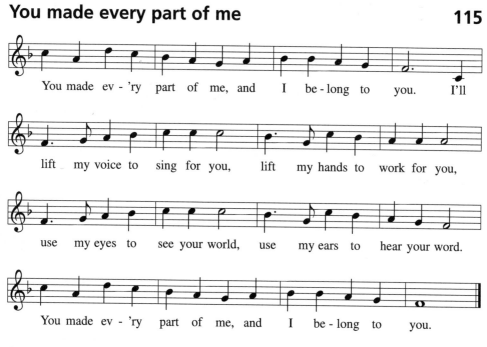

You made ev - 'ry part of me, and I be - long to you. I'll

lift my voice to sing for you, lift my hands to work for you,

use my eyes to see your world, use my ears to hear your word.

You made ev - 'ry part of me, and I be - long to you.

Text: Marie Pooler, alt. Helen Kemp
Music: Marie Pooler, alt. Helen Kemp
© 1986 Augsburg Fortress

116

Like a tree

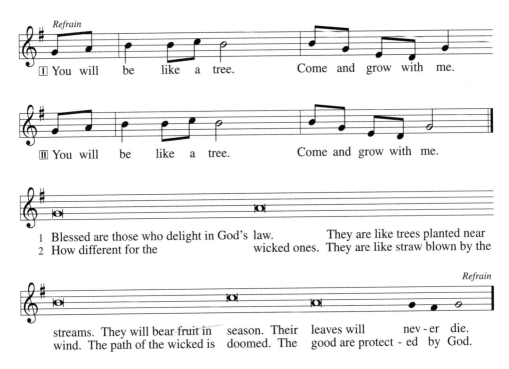

Text: Psalm 1, adapt.
Music: Julie Howard
© 1992 World Library Publications

Love is never-ending   **117**

1 We give thanks un-to you, O God of might,
2 From of old you have led your peo - ple in faith,
3 You de - liv - ered the ones who called un - to you,
4 You have o - pened the sea and brought your peo - ple through,
5 You re - mem - ber your prom - ise age to age,

for your love is nev - er - end - ing;

we give thanks un - to you, the God of gods,
you have shown your com - pas - sion, strength, and love,
from .... bond - age to free - dom, you brought them forth,
brought them in - to a land that flows with life,
you show mer - cy on those of low de - gree,

for your love is nev - er - end - ing.

Text: Psalm 136, adapt. Marty Haugen
Music: Marty Haugen
© 1987 GIA Publications

118

Two little eyes

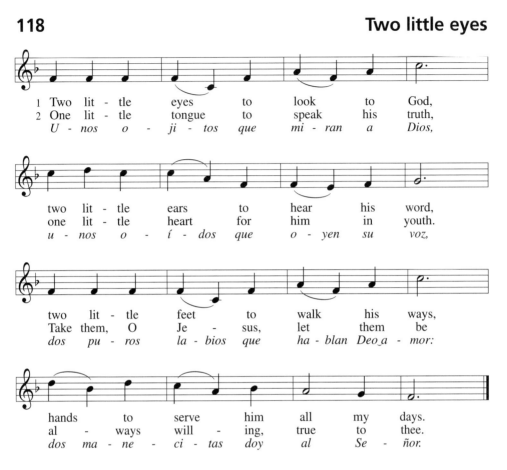

1 Two lit - tle eyes to look to God,
2 One lit - tle tongue to speak his truth,
U - nos o - ji - tos que mi - ran a Dios,

two lit - tle ears to hear his word,
one lit - tle heart for him in youth.
u - nos o - í - dos que o - yen su voz,

two lit - tle feet to walk his ways,
Take them, O Je - sus, let them be
dos pu - ros la - bios que ha - blan Deo a - mor:

hands to serve him all my days.
al - ways will - ing, true to thee.
dos ma - ne - ci - tas doy al Se - ñor.

Text: anonymous
Music: S. V. R. Ford

Earth and all stars!

119

1 Earth and all stars! Loud rush - ing plan - ets!
2 Hail, wind, and rain! Loud blow - ing snow - storm!
3 Trum - pet and pipes! Loud clash - ing cym - bals!
4 En - gines and steel! Loud pound - ing ham - mers!
5 Class-rooms and labs! Loud boil - ing test tubes!

Sing to the Lord a new song!
Sing to the Lord a new song!
Sing to the Lord a new song!
Sing to the Lord a new song!
Sing to the Lord a new song!

Oh, vic - to - ry! Loud shout - ing ar - my!
Flow - ers and trees! Loud rus - tling dry leaves!
Harp, lute, and lyre! Loud hum - ming cel - los!
Lime - stone and beams! Loud build - ing work - ers!
Ath - lete and band! Loud cheer - ing peo - ple!

Sing to the Lord a new song!
Sing to the Lord a new song!
Sing to the Lord a new song!
Sing to the Lord a new song!
Sing to the Lord a new song!

Refrain

God has done mar - vel - ous things.

I too sing prais - es with a new song!

Text: Herbert F. Brokering
Music: David N. Johnson
Text and tune © 1968 Augsburg Publishing House

120 How majestic is your name

O Lord, our Lord, how ma-jes-tic is your name in all the earth!

O Lord, our Lord, how ma-jes-tic is your name in all the earth!

O Lord, we praise your name. O Lord, we

mag-ni-fy your name, Prince of Peace, might-y God, O

Lord God Al - might - y.

Text: Michael W. Smith
Music: Michael W. Smith

I'm so glad Jesus lifted me
121

1 I'm so glad Jesus lift-ed me. I'm so glad
2 Satan had me bound, Satan had me bound,
3 When I was in trouble, When I was in trouble,

Je - sus lift - ed me. I'm so glad
Satan had me bound, Je - sus lift - ed me,
When I was in trouble,

sing-ing glo - ry, hal - le - lu - jah! Je - sus lift - ed me.

Text: African American spiritual
Music: African American spiritual

Jesus, you help
122

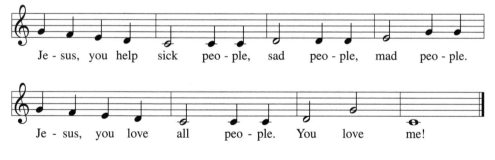

Je - sus, you help sick peo - ple, sad peo - ple, mad peo - ple.

Je - sus, you love all peo - ple. You love me!

Text: Nancy Carlson
Music: Nancy Carlson

123

When Jesus the healer

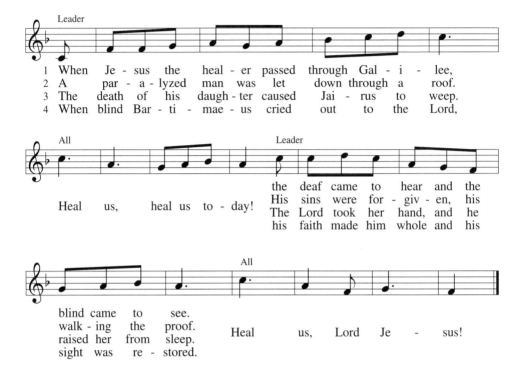

1 When Jesus the heal-er passed through Gal-i-lee,
2 A par-a-lyzed man was let down through a roof.
3 The death of his daugh-ter caused Jai-rus to weep.
4 When blind Bar-ti-mae-us cried out to the Lord,

Heal us, heal us to-day!

the deaf came to hear and the
His sins were for-giv-en, his
The Lord took her hand, and he
his faith made him whole and his

blind came to see.
walk-ing the proof.
raised her from sleep.
sight was re-stored.

Heal us, Lord Je-sus!

5 The lepers were healed and the demons cast out. Heal us, heal us today!
A bent woman straightened to laugh and to shout. Heal us, Lord Jesus.

6 The twelve were commissioned and sent out in twos, Heal us, heal us today!
to make the sick whole and to spread the good news. Heal us, Lord Jesus.

7 There's still so much sickness and suffering today. Heal us, heal us today!
We gather together for healing and pray: Heal us, Lord Jesus.

Text: Peter Smith
Music: Peter Smith
© 1978 Stainer & Bell, Ltd., admin. Hope Publishing Company

Jesus' hands were kind hands 124

1 Je - sus' hands were kind hands, do - ing good to all,
2 Take my hands, Lord Je - sus, let them work for you;

heal - ing pain and sick - ness, bless - ing chil - dren small,
make them strong and gen - tle, kind in all I do.

wash - ing ti - red feet and sav - ing those who fall;
Let me watch you, Je - sus, till I'm gen - tle too,

Je - sus' hands were kind hands, do - ing good to all.
till my hands are kind hands, quick to work for you.

Text: Margaret Cropper
Music: French traditional
Text © 1979 Stainer and Bell Ltd., admin. Hope Publishing Company

Forgive our sins as we forgive 125

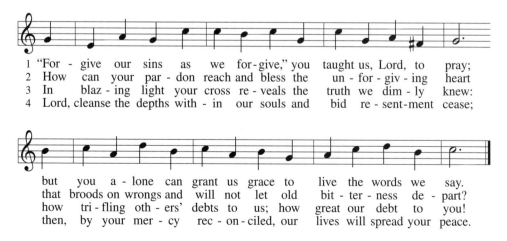

1 "For - give our sins as we for - give," you taught us, Lord, to pray;
2 How can your par - don reach and bless the un - for - giv - ing heart
3 In blaz - ing light your cross re - veals the truth we dim - ly knew:
4 Lord, cleanse the depths with - in our souls and bid re - sent - ment cease;

but you a - lone can grant us grace to live the words we say.
that broods on wrongs and will not let old bit - ter - ness de - part?
how tri - fling oth - ers' debts to us; how great our debt to you!
then, by your mer - cy rec - on - ciled, our lives will spread your peace.

Text: Rosamond E. Herklots, alt.
Music: William Croft
Text © 1969 Oxford University Press

126

Life together

Life to-geth-er, now and for-ev-er: to-geth-er for-ev-er in Je-sus' name. Life to-geth-er, now and for-ev-er: to-geth-er for-ev-er, we all pro-claim.

1 Gath-er in the Spir-it; come in from ev-'ry place. Live and learn the way of God, the sav-ing word of grace.

Refrain

Life to-geth-er, now and for-ev-er: to-geth-er for-ev-er in Je-sus' name. Life to-geth-er, now and for-ev-er: to-geth-er for-ev-er, we all pro-claim.

2 Cel - e - brate to - geth - er and share the liv - ing bread.

Go in peace to serve the Lord in ev - 'ry day a - head.

Final refrain

Life to - geth - er, now and for - ev - er: to -

geth - er for - ev - er in Je - sus' name. Life to - geth - er,

now and for - ev - er: to - geth - er for - ev - er, we all pro - claim. To -

geth - er for - ev - er, in Je - sus' name.

Text: Brian Pearson and Sherry Pearson
Music: Brian Pearson and Sherry Pearson

127　　　　　　　　　　　　　　　**Bind us together, Lord**

Refrain

Bind us to-geth-er, Lord, bind us to-geth-er with cords that

can-not be bro - ken. Bind us to-geth-er, Lord,

bind us to-geth-er, Lord; bind us to-geth-er in love.

1 There is on - ly one God. There is on - ly one King.
2 You are the fam-'ly of God. You are the prom-ise di - vine.

Refrain

There is on - ly one Bod-y; that is why we can sing.
You are God's cho-sen de-sire, . . you are the glo-rious new wine.

Text: Bob Gillman
Music: Bob Gillman
© 1977 Kingsway's Thankyou Music, admin. EMI Christian Music Publishing

Many are the lightbeams 128

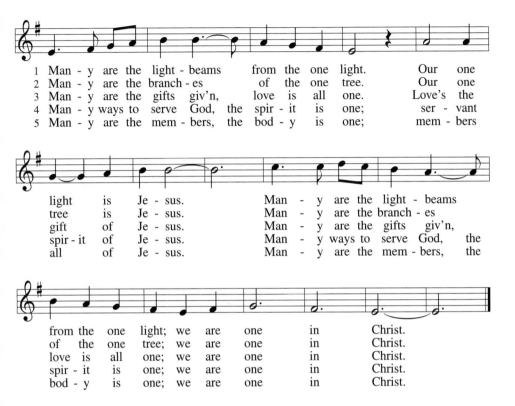

1 Man - y are the light - beams from the one light. Our one
2 Man - y are the branch - es of the one tree. Our one
3 Man - y are the gifts giv'n, love is all one. Love's the
4 Man - y ways to serve God, the spir - it is one; ser - vant
5 Man - y are the mem - bers, the bod - y is one; mem - bers

light is Je - sus. Man - y are the light - beams
tree is Je - sus. Man - y are the branch - es
gift of Je - sus. Man - y are the gifts giv'n,
spir - it of Je - sus. Man - y ways to serve God, the
all of Je - sus. Man - y are the mem - bers, the

from the one light; we are one in Christ.
of the one tree; we are one in Christ.
love is all one; we are one in Christ.
spir - it is one; we are one in Christ.
bod - y is one; we are one in Christ.

Text: Andres Frostenson, based on *De unitate ecclesiae,* Cypriam of Carthage
Music: Olle Widestrand

129 If anybody asks you who I am

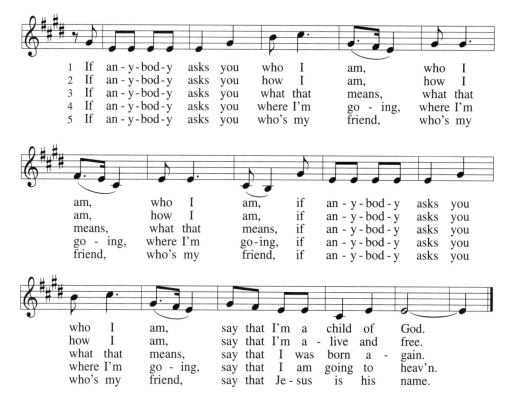

1 If an-y-bod-y asks you who I am, who I
2 If an-y-bod-y asks you how I am, how I
3 If an-y-bod-y asks you what that means, what that
4 If an-y-bod-y asks you where I'm go - ing, where I'm
5 If an-y-bod-y asks you who's my friend, who's my

am, who I am, if an-y-bod-y asks you
am, how I am, if an-y-bod-y asks you
means, what that means, if an-y-bod-y asks you
go - ing, where I'm go-ing, if an-y-bod-y asks you
friend, who's my friend, if an-y-bod-y asks you

who I am, say that I'm a child of God.
how I am, say that I'm a - live and free.
what that means, say that I was born a - gain.
where I'm go - ing, say that I am going to heav'n.
who's my friend, say that Je - sus is his name.

Text: anonymous, st. 1; Jaroslav Vajda, sts. 2-5
Music: Southern folk song
Text stanzas 2-5 © 1984 CPH Publishing

We are all one in Christ

We are all one in Christ, we are one bod - y, all one
So - mos u - no en Cris - to, so - mos u - no. So - mos

peo - ple out of man - y. man - y.
u - no, u - no so - lo. so - lo.

There is one God, and on - ly one Lord; there is one
Un so - lo Dios, un so - lo Se - ñor, u - na so - la

faith, one ho - ly love. There is one bap - tism; there is one
fe, un so - lo_a - mor. Un so - lo bau - tis - mo, un so - lo_Es-

Spir - it, who is God the com - fort - er.
pí - ri - tu, y_e - se_es el con - so - la - dor.

Text: anonymous; tr. Gerhard Cartford
Music: anonymous
Tr. © 1998 Augsburg Fortress

131   Chatter with the angels

Chat-ter with the an - gels soon in the morn - ing, chat-ter with the an - gels in that land. Chat-ter with the an - gels soon in the morn - ing, chat-ter with the an - gels, join the band. I hope to join that band and chat-ter with the an - gels all day long! I hope to join that band and chat-ter with the an - gels all day long!

Text: African American spiritual
Music: African American spiritual

Kids of the kingdom

1 Kids of the king - dom, that's what we are:
2 My name is _____, I love the Lord.
3 Kids of the king - dom, that's what we are:
4 Praise to the Fa - ther, praise to the Son,

kids of the king - dom, that's what we are.
My name is _____, I love the Lord.
kids of the king - dom, that's what we are.
praise to the Spir - it, the Three in One.

We love Je - sus, we love the Lord.
They love Je - sus, they love the Lord.
We love Je - sus, we love the Lord.
We love Je - sus, we love the Lord.

We love Je - sus, we love the Lord.
They love Je - sus, they love the Lord.
We love Je - sus, we love the Lord.
We love Je - sus, we love the Lord.

Text: Ralph Torres
Music: Ralph Torres

133

We are the church

Refrain

I am the church! You are the church!

We are the church to - geth - er! All who fol-low Je - sus,

all a-round the world, yes, we're the church to - geth - er!

1 The church is not a build - ing, the
2 We're man - y kinds of peo - ple with
3 And when the peo - ple gath - er, there's
4 At Pen - te - cost some peo - ple re -

church is not a stee - ple, the church is not a
man - y kinds of fac - es, all col - ors and all
sing - ing and there's pray - ing; there's laugh - ing and there's
ceived the Ho - ly Spir - it and told the good news

Refrain

rest - ing place; the church is a peo - ple!
a - ges too, from all times and plac - es.
cry - ing some - times, all of it say - ing,
through the world to all who would hear it.

Text: Richard Avery and Donald Marsh
Music: Richard Avery and Donald Marsh
© 1972 Hope Publishing Company

Love, love, love!

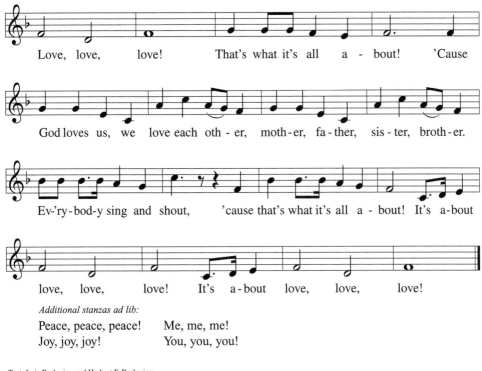

Love, love, love! That's what it's all a - bout! 'Cause

God loves us, we love each oth - er, moth - er, fa - ther, sis - ter, broth - er.

Ev-'ry-bod-y sing and shout, 'cause that's what it's all a - bout! It's a-bout

love, love, love! It's a-bout love, love, love!

Additional stanzas ad lib:

Peace, peace, peace!   Me, me, me!
Joy, joy, joy!   You, you, you!

Text: Lois Brokering and Herbert F. Brokering
Music: Lois Brokering and Herbert F. Brokering
© 1970 Augsburg Publishing House

There's a Spirit in the air 135

1 There's a Spir - it in the air, tell - ing Chris-tians ev - 'ry-where:
2 Lose your shy-ness, find your tongue; tell the worlds what God has done.
3 When be - liev - ers break the bread, when a hun - gry child is fed,
4 Still the Spir - it leads the fight, see - ing wrong and set - ting right:

praise the love that Christ re-vealed, liv - ing, work - ing, in our world.
God in Christ has come to stay. Live to - mor-row's life to - day!
praise the love that Christ re-vealed, liv - ing, work - ing, in our world.
God in Christ has come to stay. Live to - mor-row's life to - day!

Text: Brian Wren
Music: French traditional
Text © 1969, 1995 Hope Publishing Company

136 On the poor

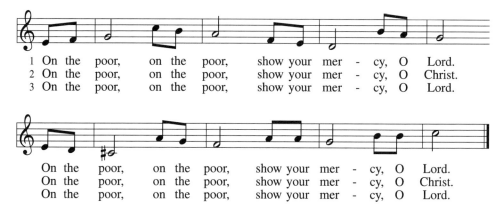

1 On the poor, on the poor, show your mer - cy, O Lord.
2 On the poor, on the poor, show your mer - cy, O Christ.
3 On the poor, on the poor, show your mer - cy, O Lord.

On the poor, on the poor, show your mer - cy, O Lord.
On the poor, on the poor, show your mer - cy, O Christ.
On the poor, on the poor, show your mer - cy, O Lord.

Text: traditional liturgical text, adapt.
Music: Paraguayan traditional

137 Make me a servant

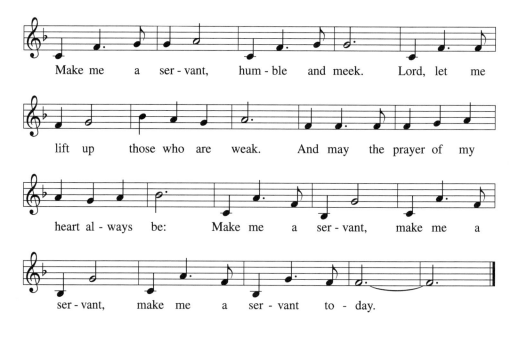

Make me a ser - vant, hum - ble and meek. Lord, let me

lift up those who are weak. And may the prayer of my

heart al - ways be: Make me a ser - vant, make me a

ser - vant, make me a ser - vant to - day.

Text: Kelly Willard
Music: Kelly Willard
© 1982 Willing Heart Music (admin. Maranatha! Music c/o The Copyright Company) and Maranatha! Music (admin. The Copyright Company)

Here I am, Lord

138

1 "I, the Lord of sea and sky, I have heard my peo-ple cry.
2 "I, the Lord of snow and rain, I have borne my peo-ple's pain.
3 "I, the Lord of wind and flame, I will tend the poor and lame.

All who dwell in deep-est sin my hand will save.
I have wept for love of them. They turn a - way.
I will set a feast for them. My hand will save.

I, who made the stars of night, I will make their dark-ness bright.
I will break their hearts of stone, give them hearts for love a - lone.
Fin-est bread I will pro-vide till their hearts be sat - is - fied.

Who will bear my light to them? Whom shall I send?"
I will speak my word to them. Whom shall I send?"
I will give my life to them. Whom shall I send?"

Refrain

Here I am, Lord. Is it I, Lord? I have heard you

call-ing in the night. I will go, Lord, if you

lead me. I will hold your peo-ple in my heart.

Text: Daniel Schutte
Music: Daniel Schutte
© 1981 Daniel L. Schutte and New Dawn Music

139

You are the seed

1 You are the seed that will grow a new sprout; you're a star that will
2 You are the flame that will light-en the dark, so re-splen-dent with
3 You are the life that will nur-ture the plant; you're the waves in a

shine in the night; you are the yeast and a small grain of salt, a
hope, faith and love; you are the shep-herds to lead the whole world to
tur-bu-lent sea; yes-ter-day's yeast is be-gin-ning to rise, a

bea-con to glow in the dark. You are the dawn that will bring a new day;
wa-ters and pas-tures of peace. "You are the friends that I chose for my-self,
new loaf of bread it will yield. There is no place for a cit-y to hide,

you're the wheat that will bear gold-en grain; you are a sting and a
you're the word that I want to pro-claim. You are the new reign of
there's no moun-tain can cov-er its might; let your light shine so that

soft, gen-tle touch, to wit-ness where-ev-er you go.
God built on rock, where jus-tice and truth are at home."
your lov-ing works give hon-or and glo-ry to God.

Refrain/Estribillo

Go, my friends, go to the world, pro - claim the great love of
Id, a - mi - gos, por el mun - do, a - nun - cian - do_el a -

God; mes - sen - gers to tell the way of life,
mor, men - sa - je - ros de la vi - da,

peace and par - don for all. Be, my friends, a loy - al wit - ness,
de la paz y_el per - dón. Sed, a - mi - gos, mis tes - ti - gos

from the dead Christ a - rose; "Lo, I'll be with you for -
de mi re - su - rrec - ción. Id lle - van - do mi pre -

ev - er - more, till the end of the world."
sen - cia; con vo - so - tros es - toy.

Text: Cesáreo Gabarain; tr. Raquel Gutiérrez-Achon and Skinner Chávez-Melo
Music: Cesáreo Gabarain

140 # Love your neighbor

Love your neigh - bor as your - self; be
gen - tle, kind and true. Love your neigh - bor as your -
self; for God has first loved you.

1 Be a friend to those who are lone - ly. Be a
2 Je - sus was a friend to the lone - ly. Je - sus

friend to those who are sad. Let your love help those who are
was a friend to the sad. Je - sus' love helped those who were

Refrain

hurt-ing. Let your love make ev - 'ry - one glad!
hurt-ing. Je - sus' love still makes ev - 'ry - one glad!

Text: Susan Eltringham
Music: Susan Eltringham

© 1993 Abingdon Press, admin. The Copyright Company

Come now, you blessed

141

1 "Come now, you bless - ed,   eat at my ta - ble,"
2 When did we see you   hun - gry or thirst - y?
3 "When you gave bread to the earth's hun - gry chil - dren,
4 Christ, when we meet you   out on life's road - ways,

said Je - sus Christ to the righ - teous a - bove.
When were you home - less, a strang - er a - lone?
when you gave wel - come to war's ref - u - gees.
look - ing to us in the fac - es of need,

"When I was hun - gry,   thirst - y, and home - less,
When did we see you   sick or in pris - on?
When you re - mem - bered those most for - got - ten,
then may we know you,   wel - come and show you

sick and in pris - on, you showed me your love."
What have we done that you call us your own?
you cared for me in the small - est of these."
love that is faith - ful in word and in deed.

Text: Ruth Duck
Music: Emily R. Brink
Text © 1992 GIA Publications, Inc.
Music © 1994 CRC Publications

142 Love God and your neighbor

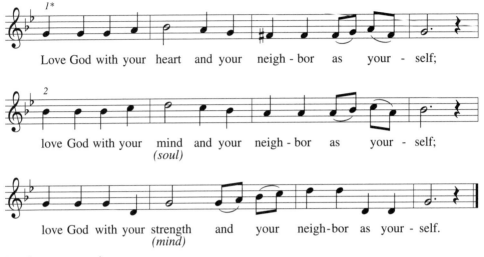

Love God with your heart and your neigh - bor as your - self;

love God with your mind and your neigh - bor as your - self;
(soul)

love God with your strength and your neigh-bor as your - self.
(mind)

*may be sung as a round

Text: from the Gospels
Music: traditional

Blest are they 143

1 Blest are they, the poor in spir-it; theirs is the king-dom of God.
2 Blest are they, the low-ly ones; they shall in-her-it the earth.
3 Blest are they . . . who show mer-cy; mer - cy shall . . be theirs.
4 Blest are they . . . who seek peace; they are the chil-dren of God.
5 Blest are you who suf-fer hate, all . . . be-cause . . of me. Re-

Blest are they, full of sor-row; they shall be con-soled.
Blest are they who hun-ger and thirst. they shall have their fill.
Blest are they, the pure of heart; they . . . shall see God.
Blest are they who suf-fer in faith; the king-dom of God is theirs.
joice, be glad, yours is the king-dom; shine . . . for all to see.

Refrain

Re - joice and be glad! Bless-ed are you; ho - ly are you!

Re - joice and be glad! Yours is the king-dom of God!

Text: David Haas
Music: David Haas
© 1985 GIA Publications, Inc.

Jesus, Jesus, let us tell you 144

1 Je - sus, Je - sus, let us tell you what we know:
2 Je - sus, Je - sus, may your Spir - it help us show
3 Je - sus, Je - sus, with your Spir - it let us go
4 Love, love, love, love, Chris - tians, this . . . is our call:

you have giv - en us your Spir - it; we love you so.
to our fam - 'ly, friends, and neigh-bors: we love you so.
to the ones who need your mer - cy; we love you so.
love our neigh-bors as our - selves, for God loves us all.

*may be sung as a round

Text: traditional, sts. 1 and 4; Bert Polman, st. 2; Joanne Hamilton, st. 3
Music: traditional
Text © 1994 CRC Publications

145

All around the world

Refrain

All a-round the world kids are pray-ing, all a-round the world pray-ing to God. Chil-dren, lift your hands and voic-es say-ing, "Hear our prayer, O God." All a-round the world!

1 Je - sus shows us how to have a con - ver - sa - tion
2 Pray for those in need and pray with - out dis - trac - tion.

with our might - y God who made the whole cre - a - tion.
Wor-ship God each day and put your prayers in ac - tion.

We can say a prayer in ev - 'ry sit - u - a - tion.
Share the news of Christ and start a chain re - ac - tion.

Refrain

God is lis - t'ning! God is there!
Make dis - ci - ples! Spread God's word!

Text: Dori Erwin Collins
Music: Dori Erwin Collins

Jesu, Jesu, fill us with your love

146

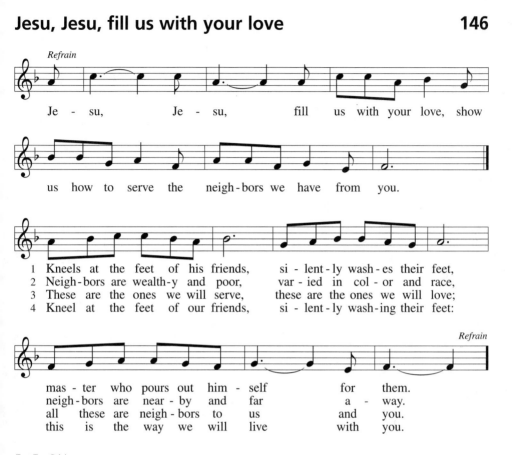

Refrain

Je - su, Je - su, fill us with your love, show

us how to serve the neigh-bors we have from you.

1 Kneels at the feet of his friends, si - lent - ly wash - es their feet,
2 Neigh-bors are wealth-y and poor, var - ied in col - or and race,
3 These are the ones we will serve, these are the ones we will love;
4 Kneel at the feet of our friends, si - lent - ly wash-ing their feet:

Refrain

mas - ter who pours out him - self for them.
neigh - bors are near - by and far a - way.
all these are neigh-bors to us and you.
this is the way we will live with you.

Text: Tom Colvin
Music: Ghanaian folk tune, adapt. Tom Colvin
© 1969 Hope Publishing Company

147

If you love me

1 If you love me, tru - ly love me, keep my com-mand-ments
2 If you love me, tru - ly love me, come now and my dis -

day by day. If you love me, tru - ly love me,
ci - ple be. If you love me, tru - ly love me,

fol - low for - ev - er in my way.
fol - low and so re - mem - ber me.

3 Through the land my peo - ple feed, al - le - lu - ia,

in their sor - row, in their need, al - le - lu - ia.

4 If you love me, tru - ly love me, in - to the world a -

rise and go. If you love me, tru - ly love me,

there ev - 'ry - where my wit - ness show.

Text: Natalie Sleeth
Music: Natalie Sleeth
© 1980 Hinshaw Music, Inc.

Let me be your servant, Jesus 148

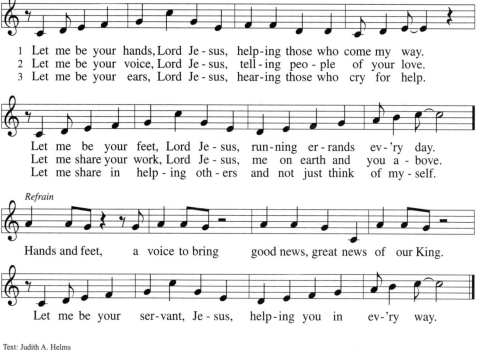

1 Let me be your hands, Lord Je-sus, help-ing those who come my way.
2 Let me be your voice, Lord Je-sus, tell-ing peo-ple of your love.
3 Let me be your ears, Lord Je-sus, hear-ing those who cry for help.

Let me be your feet, Lord Je-sus, run-ning er-rands ev-'ry day.
Let me share your work, Lord Je-sus, me on earth and you a-bove.
Let me share in help-ing oth-ers and not just think of my-self.

Refrain

Hands and feet, a voice to bring good news, great news of our King.

Let me be your ser-vant, Je-sus, help-ing you in ev-'ry way.

Text: Judith A. Helms
Music: Judith A. Helms
© 1980 Judith A. Helms

Jesus wants me for a helper 149

1 Je-sus wants me for a help-er when I work or when I play.
2 I can tell some-one, "I love you," be a friend and share my toys.
3 I can plant some pret-ty flow-ers, wash the dish-es, pull the weeds.
4 I can help to set the ta-ble, fold the clothes or make my bed.

I can show my love for Je-sus in the things I do or say.
I can show my love for Je-sus help-ing oth-er girls and boys.
I can show my love for Je-sus do-ing kind and lov-ing deeds.
I can show my love for Je-sus help-ing oth-ers as he said.

Text: Dorothy N. Schultz
Music: Dorothy N. Schultz
© 1989 CPH Publishing

150

The tiny seed

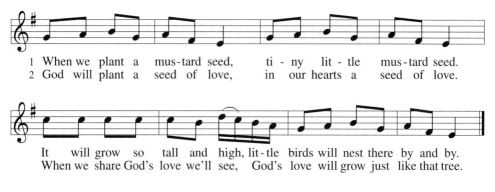

1 When we plant a mus-tard seed, ti - ny lit - tle mus-tard seed.
2 God will plant a seed of love, in our hearts a seed of love.

It will grow so tall and high, lit-tle birds will nest there by and by.
When we share God's love we'll see, God's love will grow just like that tree.

Text: Catherine Mathia and Audrey Sillick
Music: Arabic folk song
Text © 1995 Music Matters

151

We love

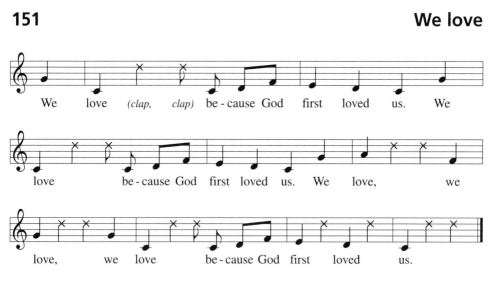

We love *(clap, clap)* be - cause God first loved us. We

love be - cause God first loved us. We love, we

love, we love be - cause God first loved us.

Text: 1 John 4:19
Music: Ann F. Price
Music © 1975 Graded Press, admin. The Copyright Company

This is my commandment

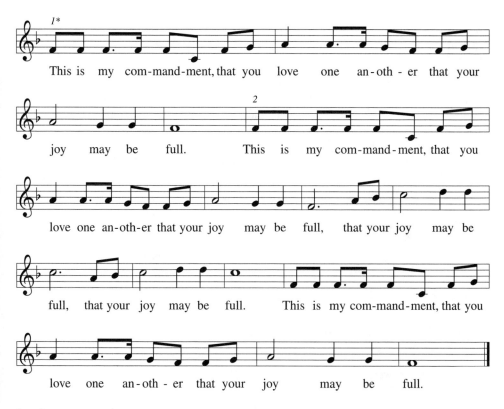

This is my com-mand-ment, that you love one an-oth-er that your joy may be full. This is my com-mand-ment, that you love one an-oth-er that your joy may be full, that your joy may be full, that your joy may be full. This is my com-mand-ment, that you love one an-oth-er that your joy may be full.

*may be sung as a round

Additional stanzas ad lib:

    This is my commandment, that you trust one another . . .
    This is my commandment, that you serve one another . . .
    This is my commandment, that you lay down your lives . . .

Text: John 15:11-12
Music: anonymous

153

When I needed a neighbor

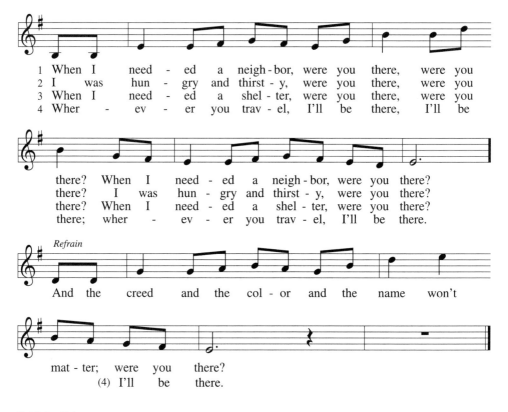

1 When I need - ed a neigh-bor, were you there, were you
2 I was hun - gry and thirst - y, were you there, were you
3 When I need - ed a shel - ter, were you there, were you
4 Wher - ev - er you trav - el, I'll be there, I'll be

there? When I need - ed a neigh-bor, were you there?
there? I was hun - gry and thirst - y, were you there?
there? When I need - ed a shel - ter, were you there?
there; wher - ev - er you trav - el, I'll be there.

Refrain

And the creed and the col - or and the name won't

mat - ter; were you there?
(4) I'll be there.

Text: Sydney Carter
Music: Sydney Carter
© 1965 Stainer & Bell Ltd., admin. Hope Publishing Company

154

I love to tell the story

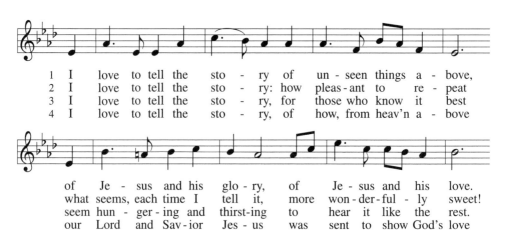

1 I love to tell the sto - ry of un - seen things a - bove,
2 I love to tell the sto - ry: how pleas - ant to re - peat
3 I love to tell the sto - ry, for those who know it best
4 I love to tell the sto - ry, of how, from heav'n a - bove

of Je - sus and his glo - ry, of Je - sus and his love.
what seems, each time I tell it, more won - der - ful - ly sweet!
seem hun - ger - ing and thirst - ing to hear it like the rest.
our Lord and Sav - ior Jes - us was sent to show God's love

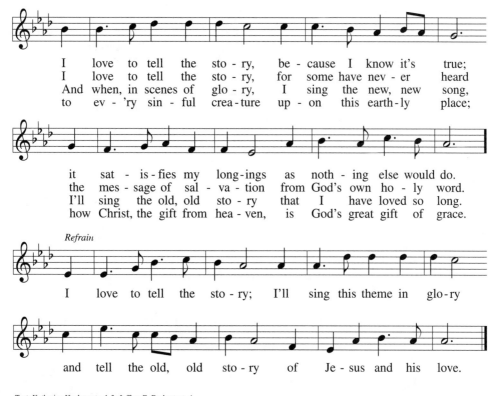

I love to tell the sto - ry, be - cause I know it's true;
I love to tell the sto - ry, for some have nev - er heard
And when, in scenes of glo - ry, I sing the new, new song,
to ev - 'ry sin - ful crea - ture up - on this earth - ly place;

it sat - is - fies my long - ings as noth - ing else would do.
the mes - sage of sal - va - tion from God's own ho - ly word.
I'll sing the old, old sto - ry that I have loved so long.
how Christ, the gift from hea - ven, is God's great gift of grace.

Refrain

I love to tell the sto - ry; I'll sing this theme in glo - ry

and tell the old, old sto - ry of Je - sus and his love.

Text: Katherine Hankey, sts. 1-3; Jeffrey E. Burkart, st. 4
Music: William G. Fischer
Text stanza 4 © Jeffrey E. Burkart

All night, all day   155

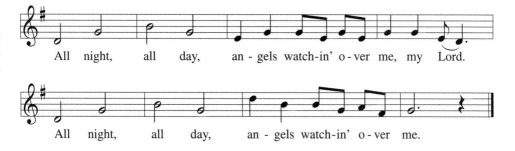

All night, all day, an - gels watch - in' o - ver me, my Lord.

All night, all day, an - gels watch - in' o - ver me.

Text: African American spiritual
Music: African American spiritual

156

One in a hundred

1 Have you heard a-bout the lit-tle lost sheep who was one in a
2 The good shep-herd went to res-cue that lamb, though his sup-per was

hun - dred? He was missed by the shep - herd who knew
cook-ing; al-though man - y hun - gry an - i -mals growled,

that he of - ten had wan-dered. Since the sheep were do - ing fine,
he just kept right on look-ing. When that lamb was found at last,

he left the nine - ty -nine to look for the lamb he knew:
the shep-herd held him fast, so glad that his search was through:

the good news is the lamb in the sto - ry is you!

Refrain

So if you're one in a hun - dred, or one in a mil - lion, or

if you're feel-ing lost as if you're one in a bil - lion, don't you know?

Je-sus loves you so! You'll nev-er, nev-er, ev-er be a - lone.

Text: John Folkening
Music: John Folkening
© 1983 Augsburg Fortress

Jesus, shepherd us

157

1 Je - sus, shep-herd us, your sheep,   when we wake and when we sleep,
2 Je - sus, shep-herd us, your sheep,   when the road is rough or steep,
3 Je - sus, shep-herd us, your sheep,   when we fall and when we leap,

when we laugh and when we weep.   Je-sus, shep-herd us, your sheep.
when the way is wide or deep   Je-sus, shep-herd us, your sheep.
in your pas-ture, safe-ly keep,   Je-sus, shep-herd us, your sheep.

Text: Wayne L. Wold
Music: Wayne L. Wold
© 1999 Augsburg Fortress

158   Give me oil in my lamp

1 Give me oil in my lamp, keep me burn - ing. Give me
2 Give me love in my heart, keep me shar - ing. Give me
3 Give me joy in my heart, keep me sing - ing. Give me
4 Give me faith in my heart, keep me pray - ing. Give me

oil in my lamp, I pray. Give me oil in my lamp, keep me
love in my heart, I pray. Give me love in my heart, keep me
joy in my heart, I pray. Give me joy in my heart, keep me
faith in my heart, I pray. Give me faith in my heart, keep me

burn - ing. Keep me burn - ing till the break of day.
shar - ing. Keep me shar - ing till the break of day.
sing - ing. Keep me sing - ing till the break of day.
pray - ing. Keep me pray - ing till the break of day.

Refrain

Sing ho-san-na, sing ho-san-na, sing ho-san-na to the King of kings!

Sing ho-san-na, sing ho-san-na, sing ho-san-na to the King!

Text: traditional
Music: traditional

I've got peace like a river

159

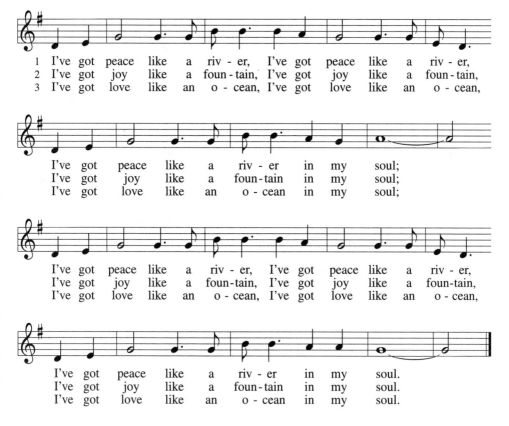

1 I've got peace like a riv-er, I've got peace like a riv-er,
2 I've got joy like a foun-tain, I've got joy like a foun-tain,
3 I've got love like an o-cean, I've got love like an o-cean,

I've got peace like a riv-er in my soul;
I've got joy like a foun-tain in my soul;
I've got love like an o-cean in my soul;

I've got peace like a riv-er, I've got peace like a riv-er,
I've got joy like a foun-tain, I've got joy like a foun-tain,
I've got love like an o-cean, I've got love like an o-cean,

I've got peace like a riv-er in my soul.
I've got joy like a foun-tain in my soul.
I've got love like an o-cean in my soul.

Text: traditional
Music: African American spiritual

160

Jesus loves me!

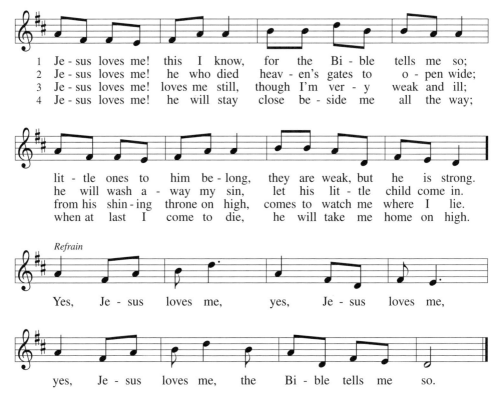

1 Je - sus loves me! this I know, for the Bi - ble tells me so;
2 Je - sus loves me! he who died heav - en's gates to o - pen wide;
3 Je - sus loves me! loves me still, though I'm ver - y weak and ill;
4 Je - sus loves me! he will stay close be - side me all the way;

lit - tle ones to him be - long, they are weak, but he is strong.
he will wash a - way my sin, let his lit - tle child come in.
from his shin - ing throne on high, comes to watch me where I lie.
when at last I come to die, he will take me home on high.

Refrain

Yes, Je - sus loves me, yes, Je - sus loves me,

yes, Je - sus loves me, the Bi - ble tells me so.

Text: Anna B. Warner
Music: William B. Bradbury

Fear not for tomorrow

1 Fear not for to - mor - row and what it may bring, but
2 Fear not for to - mor - row and what lies a - head, though
3 Fear not for to - mor - row, but lift up your voice in

trust in the Lord and o - bey. In joy or in sor - row, in
fu - ture e - vents be un - known; but wel - come the morn - ing with
an - thems of glo - ri - ous praise. Give thanks for your bless - ings and

ev - 'ry good thing, the Lord will not lead you a - stray.
cour - age in - stead, for you will not face it a - lone.
tru - ly re - joice, for God will be with you al - ways.

Refrain

God will take care of you, go ev' - ry - where with you, al - ways be

there with you day by day. God will pro - vide for you,

be as a guide to you, lov - ing - ly show you the way.

Text: Natalie Sleeth
Music: Natalie Sleeth
© 1991 Hinshaw Music, Inc.

162   # In our work and in our play

In our work and in our play God is with us ev-'ry day;

there-fore we will nev-er fear, for our lov-ing God is near.

Text: William A. Kramer
Music: Franz Schubert, adapt.
Text © 1994 CPH Publishing

163   # On eagle's wings

"And I will raise you up on ea-gle's wings, bear you on the

breath of dawn, make you to shine like the sun, and

hold you in the palm of my hand."

Text: Michael Joncas
Music: Michael Joncas
© 1979, 1991 New Dawn Music

Come, we that love the Lord

1 Come, we that love the Lord, and let our joys be known;
2 Let those re - fuse to sing who nev - er knew our God;
3 The hill of Zi - on yields a thou-sand sa - cred sweets
4 Then let our songs a-bound, and ev - 'ry tear be dry;

join in a song with sweet ac - cord, join in a song with
but chil - dren of the heav'n - ly King, but chil - dren of the
be - fore we reach the heav'n - ly fields, be - fore we reach the
we're march - ing through Em - man - uel's ground, we're march - ing through Em -

sweet ac-cord and thus sur - round the throne, and thus sur-round the throne.
heav'n-ly King may speak their joys a-broad, may speak their joys a - broad.
heav'n-ly fields, or walk the gold-en streets, or walk the gold-en streets.
man-uel's ground, to fair - er worlds on high, to fair - er worlds on high.

Refrain

We're march - ing to Zi - on, beau - ti-ful, beau - ti-ful Zi - on:

we're march - ing up-ward to Zi - on, the beau - ti-ful cit-y of God.

Text: Isaac Watts, stanzas; Robert Lowry, refrain
Music: Robert Lowry

165   **What does it mean to follow Jesus?**

Refrain

What does it mean to fol - low Je - sus? What does it mean to

go his way? What does it mean to do what he wants me to,

To stanzas ev - 'ry day?   *Last time* ev - 'ry day?

1 I can love my neigh - bor, just as Je - sus said.
2 I can say I'm sor - ry when I've done some wrong.

I can help my broth - er, see that he is fed.
I can sing his prais - es in both words and song.

I can show my sis - ter kind - ness and care.
I'll be friends with oth - ers who aren't like me.

Refrain

I can show my friends that I know how to share.
They be - long to Je - sus: we all do, you see.

Come, we that love the Lord

164

1 Come, we that love the Lord, and let our joys be known;
2 Let those re - fuse to sing who nev - er knew our God;
3 The hill of Zi - on yields a thou-sand sa - cred sweets
4 Then let our songs a - bound, and ev - 'ry tear be dry;

join in a song with sweet ac - cord, join in a song with
but chil - dren of the heav'n - ly King, but chil - dren of the
be - fore we reach the heav'n - ly fields, be - fore we reach the
we're march - ing through Em - man - uel's ground, we're march - ing through Em -

sweet ac-cord and thus sur - round the throne, and thus sur-round the throne.
heav'n-ly King may speak their joys a-broad, may speak their joys a - broad.
heav'n-ly fields, or walk the gold-en streets, or walk the gold-en streets.
man-uel's ground, to fair-er worlds on high, to fair-er worlds on high.

Refrain

We're march - ing to Zi - on, beau - ti-ful, beau-ti-ful Zi - on:

we're march-ing up-ward to Zi - on, the beau-ti-ful cit-y of God.

Text: Isaac Watts, stanzas; Robert Lowry, refrain
Music: Robert Lowry

165   **What does it mean to follow Jesus?**

Refrain

What does it mean to fol - low Je - sus? What does it mean to

go his way? What does it mean to do what he wants me to,

To stanzas

ev - 'ry day?

Last time

ev - 'ry day?

1 I can love my neigh - bor, just as Je - sus said.
2 I can say I'm sor - ry when I've done some wrong.

I can help my broth - er, see that he is fed.
I can sing his prais - es in both words and song.

I can show my sis - ter kind - ness and care.
I'll be friends with oth - ers who aren't like me.

Refrain

I can show my friends that I know how to share.
They be - long to Je - sus: we all do, you see.

Text: Lois Brokering
Music: Lois Brokering
© 1990 Lois Brokering

Walk! Walk!   166

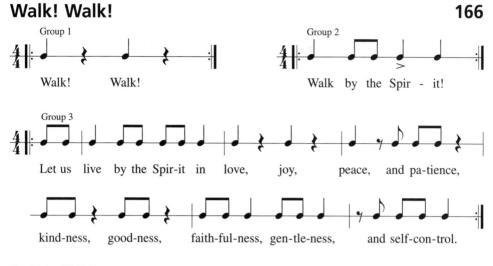

Group 1

Walk!   Walk!

Group 2

Walk by the Spir - it!

Group 3

Let us live by the Spir-it in love, joy, peace, and pa-tience,

kind-ness, good-ness, faith-ful-ness, gen-tle-ness, and self-con-trol.

Text: Galatians 5:22-23, 25
Music: Betty Ann Ramseth
© 1970 Augsburg Publishing House

Children of the heavenly Father   167

1 Chil - dren of the heav'n-ly Fa-ther safe-ly in his bo - som gath-er;
2 God his own doth tend and nour-ish, in his ho - ly courts they flour-ish.
3 Nei - ther life nor death shall ev - er from the Lord his chil-dren sev - er;
4 Though he giv - eth or he tak-eth, God his chil-dren ne'er for - sak-eth;

nest-ling bird or star in heav - en such a ref - uge ne'er was giv - en.
From all e - vil things he spares them, in his might - y arms he bears them.
un - to them his grace he show - eth, and their sor - rows all he know - eth.
his the lov - ing pur-pose sole - ly to pre-serve them pure and ho - ly.

Text: Caroline V. Sandell Berg; tr. Ernst W. Olson
Music: Swedish folk tune
Tr. © 1925 Board of Publication, Lutheran Church in America, admin. Augsburg Fortress

168   God is our refuge and strength

God is our ref-uge and strength, a ver-y pres-ent help in trou - ble.

Text: Psalm 46:1
Music: Marilyn Comer
Music © 1999 Augsburg Fortress

169   Lord of all hopefulness

1 Lord of all hope-ful-ness, Lord of all joy, whose trust, ev - er
2 Lord of all ea - ger-ness, Lord of all faith, whose strong hands were
3 Lord of all kind - li - ness, Lord of all grace, your hands swift to
4 Lord of all gen - tle-ness, Lord of all calm, whose voice is con -

child - like, no cares could de - stroy: be there at our wak - ing, and
skilled at the plane and the lathe: be there at our la - bors, and
wel - come, your arms to em - brace: be there at our hom - ing, and
tent - ment, whose pres - ence is balm: be there at our sleep - ing, and

give us, we pray, your bliss in our hearts, Lord, at the break of the day.
give us, we pray, your strength in our hearts, Lord, at the noon of the day.
give us, we pray, your love in our hearts, Lord, at the eve of the day.
give us, we pray, your peace in our hearts, Lord, at the end of the day.

Text: Jan Struther
Music: Irish folk tune
Text © 1931 Oxford University Press

I am trusting you, Lord Jesus 170

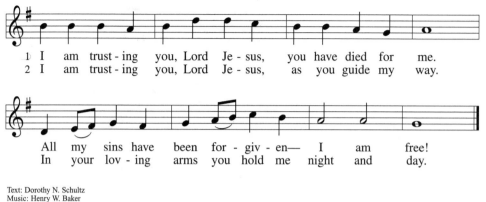

1 I am trust-ing you, Lord Je-sus, you have died for me.
2 I am trust-ing you, Lord Je-sus, as you guide my way.

All my sins have been for-giv-en— I am free!
In your lov-ing arms you hold me night and day.

Text: Dorothy N. Schultz
Music: Henry W. Baker
Text © 1989 CPH Publishing

Have no fear, little flock 171

1 Have no fear, lit-tle flock; have no fear, lit-tle
2 Have good cheer, lit-tle flock; have good cheer, lit-tle
3 Praise the Lord high a - bove; praise the Lord high a -
4 Thank-ful hearts raise to God; thank-ful hearts raise to

flock, for the Fa - ther has cho - sen to
flock, for the Fa - ther will keep you in
bove, for he stoops down to heal you, up -
God, for he stays close be - side you, in

give you the king-dom; have no fear, lit-tle flock!
his love for - ev - er; have good cheer, lit-tle flock!
lift and re - store you; praise the Lord high a - bove!
all things works with you; thank-ful hearts raise to God!

Text: Luke 12:32, st. 1; Marjorie Jillson, sts. 2-4
Music: Heinz Werner Zimmerman
© 1973 CPH Publishing

172   # The great commandments

1 You shall love the Lord with all your heart; you shall
2 You shall love your neigh-bor as your-self; you shall

love the Lord with all your soul; you shall love the
love your neigh-bor as your-self; you shall love your

Lord with all your mind; yes, heart, soul and mind.
neigh-bor as your-self; yes, you shall . . . love.

Optional responses to stanzas 1 & 2

1 Yes, I want to love the Lord with all my heart; and I
2 Yes, I want to love my neigh-bor as my-self; yes, I

want to love the Lord with all my soul; and I want to love the
want to love my neigh-bor as my-self; yes, I want to love my

Lord with all my mind; yes, heart, soul and mind.
neigh-bor as my-self; yes, I want to love.

Text: Pauline Palmer Meek
Music: Pauline Palmer Meek; arr. H. Myron Braun
© 1975 Graded Press, admin. The Copyright Company

Faith that's sure

Refrain

Faith that's sure is a rock un-shak-a-ble, plant-ed in the soil where God's
love is sown. Faith that's sure is a rock un - shak-a - ble.
Je-sus is my Lord. I'm his ver - y own! *Fine*

1 Com - pli - cat - ed ways con-fuse me. I praise my God in the
2 Come and join the cel - e - bra - tion, new in the Lord by the

sim - ple ways. Sing and dance and shout for Je - sus,
Spir - it's pow'r. Come on, friend, the Lord's a - wait - ing,

pray - ing to the Lord each and ev - 'ry day!
wait - ing for your heart this . . . ver - y hour!

Refrain

Text: Suzanne Lord
Music: Suzanne Lord
© 1995 Choristers Guild

174   **Beautiful Savior**

1 Beau - ti - ful Sav - ior, King of cre - a - tion,
2 Fair are the mead - ows, fair are the wood - lands,
3 Fair is the sun - shine, fair is the moon - light,
4 Beau - ti - ful Sav - ior, Lord of the na - tions,

Son of God and Son of Man!
robed in flow'rs of bloom - ing spring;
bright the spar - kling stars on high;
Son of God and Son of Man!

Tru - ly I'd love thee, tru - ly I'd serve thee,
Je - sus is fair - er, Je - sus is pur - er,
Je - sus shines bright - er, Je - sus shines pur - er
Glo - ry and hon - or, praise, ad - o - ra - tion,

light of my soul, my joy, my crown.
he makes our sor - rowing spir - it sing.
than all the an - gels in the sky.
now and for - ev - er - more be thine!

Text: *Gesangbuch*, Münster; tr. Joseph A. Seiss
Music: Silesian folk tune

Heleluyan

175

He - le - lu - yan, he - le - lu - yan. He - le, he - le - lu - yan.
Hal - le - lu - jah, hal - le - lu - jah. Hal - le, hal - le - lu - jah.

He - le - lu - yan, he - le - lu - yan. He - le, he - le - lu - yan.
Hal - le - lu - jah, hal - le - lu - jah. Hal - le, hal - le - lu - jah.

*may be sung as a round

Music: traditional Muscogee (Creek) Indian; transc. Charles Webb
Transcription © 1989 The United Methodist Publishing House, admin. The Copyright Company

Praise God, from whom all blessings flow

176

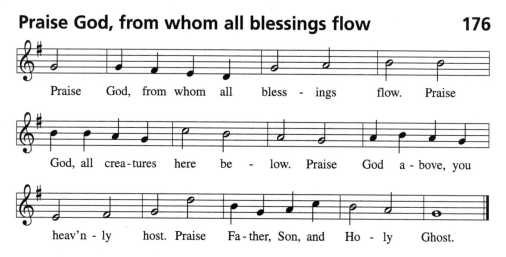

Praise God, from whom all bless - ings flow. Praise

God, all crea-tures here be - low. Praise God a - bove, you

heav'n - ly host. Praise Fa - ther, Son, and Ho - ly Ghost.

Text: Thomas Ken, alt.
Music: Louis Bourgeois

177　　　　　　　　　　　　　　　　**Halle, halle, hallelujah!**

Hal - le, hal - le, hal - le - lu - jah!

Hal - le, hal - le, hal - le - lu - jah!

Hal - le, hal - le, hal - le - lu - jah!

Hal - le - lu - jah! Hal - le - lu - jah!

Music: Caribbean traditional

178　　　　　　　　　　　　　　　　**Oh, sing to the Lord**

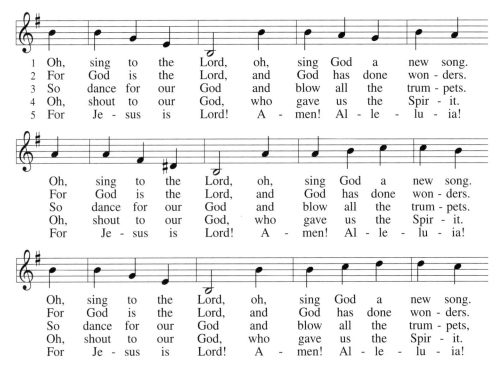

1 Oh, sing to the Lord, oh, sing God a new song.
2 For God is the Lord, and God has done won - ders.
3 So dance for our God and blow all the trum - pets.
4 Oh, shout to our God, who gave us the Spir - it.
5 For Je - sus is Lord! A - men! Al - le - lu - ia!

Oh, sing to the Lord, oh, sing God a new song.
For God is the Lord, and God has done won - ders.
So dance for our God and blow all the trum - pets.
Oh, shout to our God, who gave us the Spir - it.
For Je - sus is Lord! A - men! Al - le - lu - ia!

Oh, sing to the Lord, oh, sing God a new song.
For God is the Lord, and God has done won - ders.
So dance for our God and blow all the trum - pets,
Oh, shout to our God, who gave us the Spir - it.
For Je - sus is Lord! A - men! Al - le - lu - ia!

Oh,	sing	to	our	God,	oh,	sing	to	our	God.
Oh,	sing	to	our	God,	oh,	sing	to	our	God.
and	sing	to	our	God,	and	sing	to	our	God.
Oh,	sing	to	our	God,	oh,	sing	to	our	God.
Oh,	sing	to	our	God,	oh,	sing	to	our	God.

1 *Cantad al Señor un cántico nuevo.*
   Cantad al Señor un cántico nuevo.
   Cantad al Señor un cántico nuevo.
   ¡Cantad al Señor, cantad al Señor!

2 *Pues nuestro Señor ha hecho prodigios.*
   Pues nuestro Señor ha hecho prodigios.
   Pues nuestro Señor ha hecho prodigios.
   ¡Cantad al Señor, cantad al Señor!

Text: Brazilian folk song; tr. Gerhard Cartford
Music: Brazilian folk tune
Tr. © Gerhard Cartford

Hallelujah! Praise ye the Lord! 179

Hal-le - lu, hal-le-lu, hal-le - lu, hal-le-lu-jah! Praise ye the Lord!

Hal-le - lu, hal-le-lu, hal-le - lu, hal-le-lu-jah! Praise ye the Lord!

Praise ye the Lord! Hal-le-lu-jah! Praise ye the Lord! Hal-le-lu-jah!

Praise ye the Lord! Hal-le-lu-jah! Praise ye the Lord!

Text: traditional
Music: traditional

180

I will sing, I will sing

1. I will sing, I will sing a song un - to the Lord.
2. We will come, we will come as one be - fore the Lord.
3. If the Son, if the Son shall make . . . you . . . free,
4. They that sow in tears . . . . shall reap . . . . in . . . joy.
5. Ev - 'ry knee shall bow . . . and ev - 'ry tongue con - fess,
6. In his name, in his name we have the vic - to - ry.

I will sing, I will sing a song un - to the Lord.
We will come, we will come as one be - fore the Lord.
if the Son, if the Son shall make . . . . you . . . free,
They that sow in tears . . . . shall reap . . . . . in . . . joy.
ev - 'ry knee shall bow . . . and ev - 'ry tongue con - fess,
In his name, in his name we have the vic - to - ry.

I will sing, I will sing a song un - to the Lord.
We will come, we will come as one be - fore the Lord.
if the Son, if the Son shall make . . . . you . . . free,
They that sow in tears . . . . shall reap . . . . . in . . . joy.
ev - 'ry knee shall bow . . . and ev - 'ry tongue con - fess,
In his name, in his name we have the vic - to - ry.

Al - le - lu - ia, glo - ry to the Lord.
Al - le - lu - ia, glo - ry to the Lord.
you . . . shall be free . . . . . in - deed.
Al - le - lu - ia, glo - ry to the Lord.
that . . . Je - sus Christ . . . . is . . . Lord.
Al - le - lu - ia, glo - ry to the Lord.

Refrain

Al - le - lu, al - le - lu - ia, glo - ry to the Lord. Al - le -

lu, al-le-lu-ia, glo-ry to the Lord. Al-le-lu, al-le-lu-ia, glo-

-ry to the Lord. Al-le-lu-ia, glo-ry to the Lord.

Text: Max Dyer
Music: Max Dyer
© 1974 CELEBRATION, admin. The Copyright Company

I've got the joy, joy, joy   181

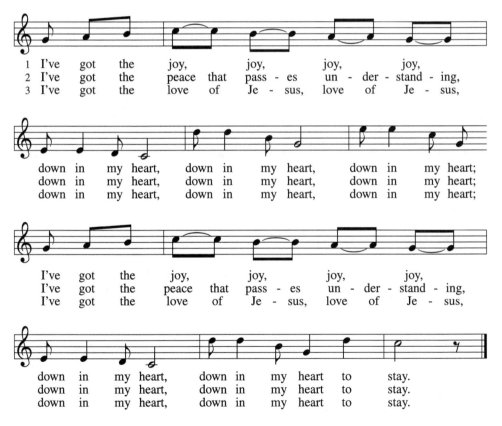

1 I've got the joy, joy, joy, joy,
2 I've got the peace that pass-es un-der-stand-ing,
3 I've got the love of Je-sus, love of Je-sus,

down in my heart, down in my heart, down in my heart;
down in my heart, down in my heart, down in my heart;
down in my heart, down in my heart, down in my heart;

I've got the joy, joy, joy, joy,
I've got the peace that pass-es un-der-stand-ing,
I've got the love of Je-sus, love of Je-sus,

down in my heart, down in my heart to stay.
down in my heart, down in my heart to stay.
down in my heart, down in my heart to stay.

Text: George W. Cooke
Music: George W. Cooke

182

Clap your hands, all you people

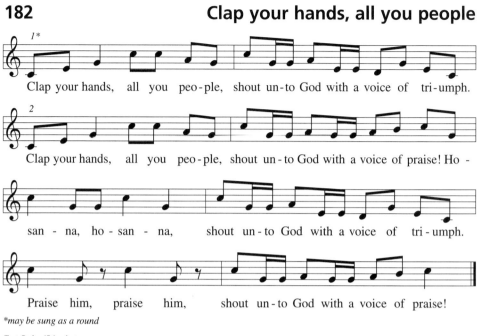

Clap your hands, all you peo-ple, shout un-to God with a voice of tri-umph.

Clap your hands, all you peo-ple, shout un-to God with a voice of praise! Ho -

san - na, ho - san - na, shout un-to God with a voice of tri-umph.

Praise him, praise him, shout un-to God with a voice of praise!

*may be sung as a round

Text: Psalm 47:1, adapt.
Music: Jimmy Owens
© 1972 Lexicon Music, Inc.

183

Sing alleluia

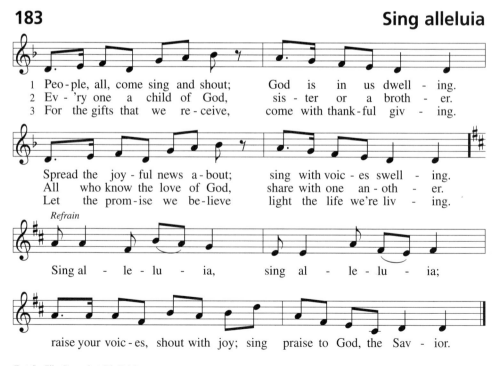

1 Peo-ple, all, come sing and shout; God is in us dwell - ing.
2 Ev - 'ry one a child of God, sis - ter or a broth - er.
3 For the gifts that we re-ceive, come with thank-ful giv - ing.

Spread the joy-ful news a-bout; sing with voic - es swell - ing.
All who know the love of God, share with one an - oth - er.
Let the prom-ise we be-lieve light the life we're liv - ing.

Refrain

Sing al - le - lu - ia, sing al - le - lu - ia;

raise your voic - es, shout with joy; sing praise to God, the Sav - ior.

Text: Sue Ellen Page; adapt. Eric D. Johnson
Music: Sue Ellen Page
© 1968, 1986 Choristers Guild

One, two, three

184

One, two, three, the Ho-ly Trin-i-ty. It shall be for

all e-ter-ni-ty. Three in one and one in three,

it's part of God's mys-ter-y. One, two, three, the Ho-ly Trin-i-ty.

Text: Pamela L. Hughes
Music: Pamela L. Hughes
© 1995 Living the Good News, Inc.

Oh, for a thousand tongues to sing

185

1 Oh, for a thou-sand tongues to sing my great re-deem-er's praise,
2 The name of Je-sus charms our fears and bids our sor-rows cease,
3 To God all glo-ry, praise, and love be now and ev-er giv'n

the glo-ries of my God and king, the tri-umphs of his grace!
sings mu-sic in the sin-ner's ears, brings life and health and peace.
by saints be-low and saints a-bove, the church in earth and heav'n.

Text: Charles Wesley
Music: Carl G. Gläser

186

Make a glad noise to the Lord

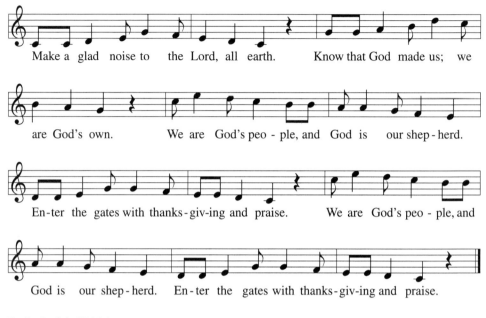

Make a glad noise to the Lord, all earth. Know that God made us; we

are God's own. We are God's peo - ple, and God is our shep - herd.

En - ter the gates with thanks - giv - ing and praise. We are God's peo - ple, and

God is our shep - herd. En - ter the gates with thanks - giv - ing and praise.

Text: based on Psalm 100:1, 3, 4
Music: Czechoslovakian folk song
Text © 1969 Augsburg Publishing House

187

Alleluia

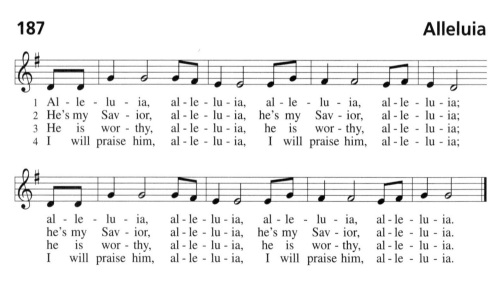

1 Al - le - lu - ia, al - le - lu - ia, al - le - lu - ia, al - le - lu - ia;
2 He's my Sav - ior, al - le - lu - ia, he's my Sav - ior, al - le - lu - ia;
3 He is wor - thy, al - le - lu - ia, he is wor - thy, al - le - lu - ia;
4 I will praise him, al - le - lu - ia, I will praise him, al - le - lu - ia;

al - le - lu - ia, al - le - lu - ia, al - le - lu - ia, al - le - lu - ia.
he's my Sav - ior, al - le - lu - ia, he's my Sav - ior, al - le - lu - ia.
he is wor - thy, al - le - lu - ia, he is wor - thy, al - le - lu - ia.
I will praise him, al - le - lu - ia, I will praise him, al - le - lu - ia.

Text: Jerry Sinclair
Music: Jerry Sinclair
© 1972 Manna Music, Inc

Alleluia   188

Al - le - lu - ia,   al - le - lu - ia!   Al - le - lu - ia,

al - le - lu - ia,   al - le - lu - ia!

Text: traditional
Music: *Geistliche Kirchengesäng*, Köln

Rejoice in the Lord always   189

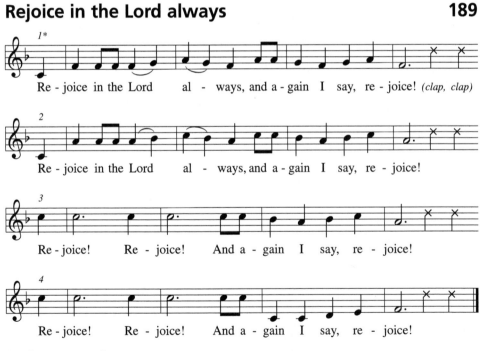

1*
Re - joice in the Lord   al - ways, and a - gain I say, re - joice! *(clap, clap)*

2
Re - joice in the Lord   al - ways, and a - gain I say, re - joice!

3
Re - joice!   Re - joice!   And a - gain I say, re - joice!

4
Re - joice!   Re - joice!   And a - gain I say, re - joice!

may be sung as a round

Text: Philippians 4:4
Music: traditional

Acknowledgments and copyright holders

Compiler: Marilyn Comer

Reviewers: Kari Anderson, Carol Benson, Sherilyn Bergdorff, Lois Brokering, Martha Fisher, Cindy Fisher-Bronin, Nick Fisher-Bronin, Ronald A. Nelson, Scott Weidler, Wayne L. Wold

Augsburg Fortress staff: Norma Aamodt-Nelson, Suzanne Burke, Carol Carver, D. Foy Christopherson, Ann Delgehausen, Ryan French, Charles Humphrey, Lynn Joyce Hunter, Lynette Johnson, Aaron Koelman, Rebecca Lowe, David Meyer, Kristine Oberg, Linda Parriott, Rachel Riensche, Martin A. Seltz, Frank Stoldt, Eric Vollen, Mark Weiler

Cover art and design: Tanja Butler, Circus Design

Music engraving: Thomas Schaller, Mensura Music Preparation

Copyediting and music preparation: Becky Brantner-Christiansen, J. David Moore, Dean Niquette, Lani Willis

Material from the following sources is acknowledged: *Praying Together,* © 1988 English Language Liturgical Consultation: texts of "Glory to God in the highest" (#20), "Lamb of God" (#46), and "Our Father in heaven" (#96).

Copyright acknowledgment: The publisher gratefully acknowledges all copyright holders who have granted permission to reproduce copyrighted materials in this book. Every effort has been made to determine the owner(s) and/or administrator(s) of each copyright and to secure needed permission. The publisher will, upon written notice, make necessary corrections in subsequent printings.

Permission information: Permission to reproduce copyrighted words or music contained in this book must be obtained from the copyright holder(s) of that material. A list of the major copyright holders represented in this book follows, with information current as of the year of publication of *LifeSongs.* Some of the songs may be covered under one or more major licensing agencies, but because this status may change from time to time, it is best to verify this information with the copyright holder or licensing agency at the time of use. For contact information of copyright holders not listed here or for further copyright information, please contact Augsburg Fortress.

AUGSBURG FORTRESS PUBLISHERS
PO Box 1209
Minneapolis, MN 55440-1209
(800) 421-0239
(612) 330-3252 FAX

AF-STIFTELSEN
Psalm Och Sang
Box 512 34300
Almhult Sweden

CHORISTERS GUILD
2834 West Kingsley Road
Garland, TX 75041-2498
(972) 271-1521
(972) 840-3113 FAX

THE COPYRIGHT COMPANY
40 Music Square East
Nashville, TN 37203
(615) 244-5588
(615) 244-5591 FAX

CRC PUBLICATIONS
2850 Kalamazoo Ave. SE
Grand Rapids, MI 49560
(616) 246-0785
(616) 246-0834 FAX

CPH PUBLISHING
3558 South Jefferson Avenue
St. Louis, MO 63118
(800) 325-0191
(314) 268-1329 FAX

DAVID HIGHAM ASSOCIATES, LTD.
5-8 Lower John Street
Golden Square
London W1R 4HA UK
011-44-171-437-7888
011-44-171-437-1072 FAX

EMI CHRISTIAN MUSIC PUBLISHING
101 Winners Circle
PO Box 5085
Brentwood, TN 37024-5085
(615) 371-4400
(615) 371-6897 FAX

FREDERICK HARRIS CO., LTD.
2250 Military Road
Tonawanda, NY 14150
(905) 501-1595
(905) 501-0929 FAX

GIA PUBLICATIONS, INC.
7404 South Mason Avenue
Chicago, IL 60638
(800) 442-1358
(708) 496-3828 FAX

HINSHAW MUSIC, INC.
Box 470
Chapel Hill, NC 27514
(919) 933-1691
(919) 967-3399 FAX

HOPE PUBLISHING COMPANY
380 South Main Place
Carol Stream, IL 60188
(800) 323-1049
(630) 665-2552

ICEL
1522 K Street Northwest, Suite 1000
Washington, DC 20005
(202) 347-0800
(202) 347-1839 FAX

INTEGRITY MUSIC, INC.
1000 Cody Road
Mobile, AL 36695
(334) 633-9000
(334) 633-5202 FAX

ISEDET
Camacuá 282
Buenos Aires 1406 Argentina
011-54-1-632-5039
011-54-1-633-2825 FAX

LEXICON MUSIC INC., USA,
M.P.I. LTD
75 High Street
Needham Market
Suffolk IP6 8AN England

LIVING THE GOOD NEWS, INC.
600 Grant Street, Suite 400
Denver, CO 80203-3524
(303) 832-4427

LUTHERAN THEOLOGICAL
COLLEGE AT MAKUMIRA
(Contact Augsburg Fortress for permission, or)
PO Box 55
Usa River (near Arusha)
Tanzania, East Africa
011-25-557-3858 FAX

LUTHERAN WORLD FEDERATION
Box 2100
150 route de Ferney
CH1211 Geneva 2 Switzerland
011-41-22-791-6360
011-41-22-798-8616 FAX

MANNA MUSIC, INC.
Box 218
35255 Brooten Road
Pacific City, OR 97135
(503) 965-6112
(503) 965-6880 FAX

MORNINGSTAR MUSIC PUBLISHERS
1727 Larkin Williams Road
Fenton, MO 63026-2024
(800) 647-2117
(314) 647-2777 FAX

MUSIC MATTERS, INC.
409 Blandwood Avenue
Greensboro, NC 27401-2705
(800) 216-6864

NEW DAWN MUSIC
5536 NE Hassalo PO Box 18030
Portland, OR 97218-0030
(800) 548-8749
(503) 282-3486 FAX

OCP PUBLICATIONS
5536 NE Hassalo PO Box 18030
Portland, OR 97218-0030
(800) 548-8749
(503) 282-3486 FAX

OXFORD UNIVERSITY PRESS
Walton Street
Oxford OX2 6DP England
011-44-186-555-6767
011-44-186-526-7749 FAX

PRINCE OF PEACE PUBLISHING,
CHANGING CHURCH, INC.
200 East Nicollet Blvd
Burnsville, MN 55337
(612) 435-8107

SELAH PUBLISHING COMPANY
58 Pearl Street
Box 3037
Kingston, NY 12401-0902
(914) 338-2816
(914) 338-2991 FAX

WALT DISNEY COMPANY
3900 West Alameda Street
Burbank, CA 91505
818-569-3270
818-845-9705 FAX

WORLD COUNCIL OF CHURCHES
150 route de Ferney
PO Box 2100
CH1211 Geneva 2 Switzerland
011-41-22-791-6111
011-41-22-798-1346 FAX

WORLD LIBRARY PUBLICATIONS
A Division of J. S. Paluch Company,
Inc.
3825 North Willow Road
Schiller Park, IL 60176-9936
(800) 621-5197
(888) 957-3291

First lines and common titles